The Red Earth

Ohio University Research in International Studies

This series of publications on Africa, Latin America, Southeast Asia, and Global and Comparative Studies is designed to present significant research, translation, and opinion to area specialists and to a wide community of persons interested in world affairs. The editors seek manuscripts of quality on any subject and can usually make a decision regarding publication within three months of receipt of the original work. Production methods generally permit a work to appear within one year of acceptance. The editors work closely with authors to produce high-quality books. The series appears in a paperback format and is distributed worldwide. For more information, consult the Ohio University Press website, ohioswallow.com.

Books in the Ohio University Research in International Studies series are published by Ohio University Press in association with the Center for International Studies. The views expressed in individual volumes are those of the authors and should not be considered to represent the policies or beliefs of the Center for International Studies, Ohio University Press, or Ohio University.

The Red Earth is the fifth volume in the Translation Series of the Southeast Asia Translations Project Group. It is published in cooperation with the Center for International Studies, Ohio University, as Number 66 in the Center's Research in International Studies, Southeast Asia Series.

The Red Earth

A Vietnamese Memoir of Life on a Colonial Rubber Plantation

by Tran Tu Binh

as told to Ha An

TRANSLATED BY JOHN SPRAGENS, JR.

EDITED AND INTRODUCED BY DAVID G. MARR

OHIO UNIVERSITY CENTER IN INTERNATIONAL STUDIES
RESEARCH IN INTERNATIONAL STUDIES
CENTER FOR SOUTHEAST ASIAN STUDIES
SOUTHEAST ASIA SERIES NUMBER 66
OHIO UNIVERSITY PRESS
ATHENS

To obtain permission to quote, reprint, or otherwise reproduce or distribute
material from Ohio University Press publications, please contact our rights and
permissions department at (740) 593-1154 or (740) 593-4536 (fax).
www.ohioswallow.com

Printed in the United States of America
The books in the Ohio University Research in International Studies Series
are printed on acid-free paper ∞ ™

Library of Congress Cataloging-in-Publication Data
Tran, Tu Binh, 1907–
    The red earth
    (Papers in International studies. Southeast Asia series; no. 66
    ISBN 0-89680-119-5
    1. Tran, Tu Binh, 1907–. 2. Vietnam-Politics and
government—1858–1945. 3. Plantations—Vietnam. 4. Revolutionists—
Vietnam—Biography. 5. Communists—Vietnam—Biography.
I. Ha, An. II. Marr, David G. III. Title
    IV. Series.

DS556.83.T7 A3613 1984
959.7'03'0924 [B]   84-20616
                                        CIP

Contents

INTRODUCTION

Tran Tu Binh was born May 1907 in an all-Catholic village in Ha-nam Province in the Red River delta of northern Vietnam. His father sustained the family by collecting and selling manure, perhaps the lowliest occupation in the village. His mother managed nevertheless to scrape together enough money to enroll Tran Tu Binh at a seminary, where he disappointed both of them in 1926 by being expelled for publicly mourning the death of Phan Chu Trinh, a prominent Vietnamese scholar-patriot. At that moment, without yet knowing it, Tran Tu Binh joined the ranks of the young intelligentsia, a group destined to play a critical role in modern Vietnamese history.

As narrated with piquancy and verve in this autobiography, Tran Tu Binh spent the next year as an itinerant Bible teacher, then signed up to labor on a rubber plantation in the distant red-earth region of southern Vietnam [Cochinchina]. Although he 'doesn't say so, this was surely another severe blow to the family. After all, even without any school diploma, Tran Tu Binh could have found a respectable job as village clerk, 'landlord's agent, or shopkeeper simply because he knew how to speak and read French as well as Vietnamese. Instead he was determined to break away, to seek adventure, to test his physical and spiritual powers on totally unfamiliar terrain. He was also vaguely familiar with the Leninist concept of "proletarianization," whereby young intellectuals immersed themselves in a working-class environment in order to engineer eventually the overthrow of both foreign imperialists and native landlords.

Even before boarding the French ship *Dorier* that was to take him south, Tran Tu Binh became embroiled in a confrontation with plantation recruiting agents who had defrauded hundreds of his illiterate fellow workers. Because the agents feared that many contract workers might simply pack up and return home, some satisfaction was obtained; however, the atmosphere became more ominous the further they traveled. When the ship docked in Saigon, workers were driven ashore like cattle and a spokesman was badly beaten for daring to complain. After being trucked to a tropical forest location 120 kilometers north of Saigon, Tran Tu Binh found himself in truly appalling physical and psychological circumstances.

Phu Rieng was one of about twenty-five French rubber plantations that stretched in a three-hundred-kilometer band from the South China Sea to the Mekong River in Cambodia. From before World War I the colonial government had allocated huge blocks of forest land to metropolitan corporations; from 1920 on, large amounts of capital became available to construct roads, nurture rubber seedlings, clear land, and plant saplings. Unlike the British in Malaya, who imported Indian or Chinese nationals to develop rubber estates, the French decided to use indigenous labor. However, they soon discovered that the proto-Indonesian tribespeople who normally wandered this region were quite unsuited to plantation work. Ethnic Vietnamese who resided in and around Saigon, although they might be lured on a seasonal basis, preferred not to sign longer-term contracts. Besides, they were close enough to home to walk away if conditions proved intolerable. These facts led French rubber companies, with colonial government encouragement and assistance, to focus increasingly on recruiting contract laborers from the heavily populated Red River delta provinces far to the north. From a mere 3,022 contract laborers on southern rubber plantations in 1922, the number increased ten times to 30,637 in 1930.[1] Tran Tu Binh was one of the 17,606 who arrived in 1927 alone.

Today's reader will perhaps be skeptical of Tran Tu Binh's "hell-on-earth" description of Phu Rieng. Admittedly, he employs poetic license on occasion. For example, one finds it hard to believe that so many husbands died of humiliation and heartbreak after their wives had been raped by plantation overseers. Nor does it seem likely that all pregnancies at Phu Rieng resulted in stillbirths. On the other hand, many of Tran Tu Binh's grim assertions are confirmed in confidential reports that colonial administrators forwarded to Paris, and which are now available for study in the Archives Nationales de France (Section Outre-Mer). For example, the minister of colonies is told that 17 percent of Phu Rieng workers died in 1927, probably a conservative figure, since the plantation supervisory staff had reason to cover up some losses. Then, too, Tran Tu Binh's characterization of Triair, the plantation director, as particularly brutal is corroborated in a report of the governor general to Paris.[2] Overall, Tran's account of plantation life may be assessed as exaggerated in tone, yet essentially reliable in substance.

One theme pervades *The Red Earth:* the existence of a bitter test of wills between exploiter and exploited. We see it first in Tran Tu Binh's confrontation with the Canadian priest, Father Quy, which culminates in a bit of Jesuit-like rhetorical jousting in a Hanoi prison eighteen years later. We see it again in the author's argument with the captain of the *Dorier* en route from Haiphong to Saigon. Most important, we are witness to the ruthless, persistent efforts of the Phu Rieng supervisory staff to tear down the psychological defenses of Vietnamese workers in order better to control them. For at least one year these tactics—akin to those of slave masters, prison workers, and drill sergeants since time immemorial—enjoy considerable success. Workers are clearly disoriented and demoralized. Gradually, however, some workers recover internal poise, improvise protective tactics, organize quietly, and plan countermeasures. Ironically, they are assisted by Triair's less brutal successor, Vasser, who allows them to form a variety of sporting, cultural, and religious groups.

Because Tran Tu Binh can understand French, he is more aware than most of the nonphysical aspects of oppression. He points out how each plantation staff member styles himself "master" and demands that workers use that form of address. Each "master" refers to the Vietnamese as children or animals. One senses that such verbal abuse rankles Tran Tu Binh even more than blows from the truncheon. It follows that much of what he and his comrades do in response is an attempt to prove to themselves, and perhaps to the French as well, that they are resourceful adults who know how to take destiny in hand.

Tran Tu Binh's knowledge of French often led his fellow workers to thrust him forward as spokesman, an inherently dangerous position. However, it also led to his being employed as an orderly at the plantation clinic, a "soft" job (for which he continued to be apologetic) clearly enabling him to study the enemy more carefully and to make many friends among the worker patients. When a member of Ho Chi Minh's Revolutionary Youth League came secretly to Phu Rieng he naturally sounded out the clever medical orderly. Soon a four-person cell was formed, followed eventually by a Communist party branch with Tran Tu Binh in charge of organizing a security unit.

Although there was scant opportunity for formal political instruction, plantation workers at Phu Rieng were not devoid of revolutionary experience. They had already learned, for example, that to swear a blood oath and split open the head of a hated French overseer brought a few moments of satisfaction, but also provoked terrible retaliation. On the other hand, they had discovered the futility of relying on colonial justice to punish the wicked. In one specific case that advanced as far as a court in Bien-hoa, an overseer found guilty of negligent manslaughter was sentenced to pay a token five piasters to the victim's widow. Workers also leaked stories to Saigon newspapers about the dire conditions at Phu Rieng. They devised a method to sabotage rubber saplings without being discovered. Although such initiatives did induce the French to make minor concessions, the basic system of exploitation remained fixed.

The new Communist party's objectives at Phu Rieng were to heighten class consciousness among plantation workers, to build an organization implicitly competing for power with the Michelin company hierarchy, and to link local with regional and national struggles. From Tran Tu Binh's account, it seems that by 1929 Phu Rieng laborers were able to react quickly to some of the more flagrant cases of physical abuse and to gain redress from the plantation director. Then they went a step further, demanding and receiving better food, better medical care, and boiled water to drink at work sites. Excited by these gains, workers began to look toward a general strike.

Recalling events thirty-four years later, Tran Tu Binh still manages to convey the millenarian excitement that gripped Phu Rieng workers in early 1930. The strike was set to coincide with the Vietnamese Lunar New Year (*Tet*), always a time of high emotion and spiritual renewal. Most workers probably had in mind overturning the evil masters, enjoying a huge feast, and then proceeding to operate the plantation themselves pending a new deal from the authorities. Some workers sharpened weapons in expectation of an armed uprising. Tran Tu Binh makes it clear that the local Communist party branch (of which he had become secretary) was of no mind to try to hold back the movement, although it had no authorization from higher echelons to proceed beyond a simple strike. It did engage in rudimentary contingency planning, ensuring that workers established hidden food caches, and making a pact with some of the local tribespeople whereby the latter promised not to serve as strikebreakers for the French.

The plantation director, Soumagnac, seems to have been poorly prepared for what happened from the first day of Tet (30 January 1930) onward. Not until his office was surrounded by angry workers three days later did he telephone the nearest military post for reinforcements. Somehow workers managed to disarm seven soldiers and send an entire platoon into retreat. This forced Soumagnac to sign a paper agreeing to all the workers' demands, after which the festival of revolution began, complete with demonstrations, red flags, speeches, singing of the "International," rifle volleys in the air, burning of office files, traditional opera performances, and a torchlight banquet. All supervisory staff were allowed to flee the plantation.

Throughout the night of 2–3 February 1930, the Communist party branch met apart from the festivities debating what should be done next. To resist incoming troops meant bloodshed, defeat, and repression. Not to resist meant deflation of the movement, probable demoralization of the workers. Similar dilemmas were encountered a few months later by party members in a number of other locations, most notably the provinces of Nghe An and Ha Tinh. The manner in which Tran Tu Binh and comrades dealt with their own "moment of truth" provides valuable insight into a much larger question of revolutionary strategy and tactics.

Whatever they decided, the Phu Rieng strike leaders were likely to be killed or captured. Tran Tu Binh was arrested, tried, and sentenced to five years on the infamous Con-Son prison island. There, like so many other radical Vietnamese intellectuals, his systematic training as a Marxist-Leninist began. Upon release the party designated him secretary of his home district committee, then in 1939 promoted him to be Ha-nam province secretary. As a member of the party's Northern Region Committee he helped engineer the general uprising in Hanoi in August 1945. Subsequently, he was deputy secretary of the party's Central Military Committee, commander of the army's military academy, and chief inspector of the Vietnam People's Armed Forces. In 1959 he was appointed ambassador to China, and the following year was made a member of the party's Central Committee. Tran Tu Binh died in February 1967 and was honored posthumously with a medal befitting his long service to party, state and army.[3]

The Red Earth is a straightforward account of how one Vietnamese youth became involved in revolutionary politics, was tested amidst the most difficult conditions imaginable, and not only survived, but also gained the obvious respect of his peers. Nevertheless, readers will be aware that a number of Marxist-Leninist didactic points are being made as the story progresses. Three times, for example, Tran Tu Binh asserts that the more people are oppressed the more they will struggle, a theme that Ho Chi Minh stressed constantly, and that was also meant to be applied by Vietnamese readers in 1964 to the growing threat posed by the United States. The feasibility of ethnic Vietnamese (*Kinh*) and highland minority

(*Thuong*) peoples joining to fight a common foe is highlighted for the same reason. Only passing mention is given to international proletarian solidarity, since that sentiment was much weaker in 1964 than it had been in 1930. Naturally "the Communist party" is given credit at the end for every significant achievement, although the narrative itself suggests no such thing.

The Red Earth is one of more than a hundred memoirs published since 1960 by veterans of the 1925–45 struggles in Vietnam. Like many other busy luminaries, Tran Tu Binh relied to some degree on a ghost writer, Ha An by name. Although it is impossible to know how Ha An influenced the narrative, a comparison of this book with certain others suggests that Tran Tu Binh was entirely in control. The story has a liveliness and sense of milieu that only one who actually experienced the events could provide. If the story is excessively dramatic in places, this stems from spontaneous feelings of the participant, not the stylistic devices of a literary cadre. In short, we have here an authentic, edifying, and eminently readable autobiography.

David G. Marr

The Red Earth

by Tran Tu Binh

as told to Ha An

A FORK IN THE ROAD

At the end of 1926 I was expelled from the Hoang Nguyen seminary. My parents were distressed by the news. My father was from Tien-dong (in Binh-luc District, Ha-nam Province), a village which had long been entirely Catholic. So it is easy to understand why my parents were angry when they heard that their son had been expelled from the seminary for "troublemaking." But what was this crime? Is it reasonable to call taking part in a struggle to protect our people's honor "troublemaking"? This is how it happened. The summer before, I had gone to Nam-dinh and Ha-noi during the school vacation. On this occasion relatives gave me some modern literature (*tan thu*) to read.[1] Reading these selections clarified many things for me. As a result, I joined with my compatriots in a tumultuous struggle demanding that the imperialists free Phan Boi Chau. At the end of summer I returned to the seminary, and the mere sight of the seminary transformed me. Echoes of the patriotic movement had burst through the walls of the Hoang Nguyen seminary. The revolutionary seed had fallen on good ground.

In the Hoang Nguyen seminary we were stifled, ill-treated, and scorned. At that time the head of the seminary was Father Quy, a Canadian priest. Father Quy did not practice what he preached. He enjoyed himself like a prince. His meals meant the table filled with an abundance of meat and fish, more than he could possibly eat. Night after night he could not get to sleep without a woman. All the same, when Father Quy stood to celebrate mass he watched over everything with extraordinary solemnity. Behind him the candles were dazzling. Father Quy, majestically tall and heavyset, held the holy bread and sacramental wine and raised his voice: "This is my body. . . . This is my blood. . . ." Down below we had to bow our heads and murmur our prayers with the utmost respect.

Being inquisitive and stubborn by nature, I always had to hold something in my hand and see it with my own eyes before I would believe it. When I heard what Father Quy said, I was very dubious. I looked for a way to see if Father Quy's sacramental bread and wine were really so amazing and precious. One day, when Father Quy was away, I quickly went and snatched the key to the sacristy, sneaked in and opened the chest holding the bread and wine. I couldn't tell any difference between that bread and wine and ordinary bread and wine. I tried eating and drinking some, and still couldn't see how they were different from plain bread and wine. So Father Quy was just bluffing everyone. Then I ate my fill of holy bread, because at the seminary we had a very austere diet. Our meals consisted of a dish of tough spinach and rice stretched with two parts corn to each part stale rice. Meat and fish were scarce as gold.

After the incident with the sacramental bread and wine, I became suspicious of everything else. I paid careful attention and learned another interesting thing. At that time, Catholics in the area often received holy water from Father Quy to take home to exorcize demons. This holy water was nothing but plain water drawn from the well, to which Father Quy added a bit of table salt to give it an unusual taste. But if they wanted Father Quy to give them the holy water, people had to have money or bamboo sacramental objects. Only then would he dispense a tiny bit to each person, in a bottle the size of a bottle of salve.

That was one thing. The way we studied is also worth mentioning. The books we studied were all terrifying. One book that I still remember was called *Where Will You Go When You Die?* It was filled with horrible tales: hellfire, demons, stocks and chains, places so hot you would almost die of thirst but never get to drink. This was not the sort of book which would cause people to believe in God, but one to make them fear the judgment and punishment of God. When I could no longer believe in this kind of book, I had to look for my beliefs elsewhere. I had to search for my own road. That was my main crime.

That is looking at it in terms of religious belief. There was also the fact that Father Quy had gravely offended our patriotic sensitivities. Father Quy had an extraordinarily hateful attitude. He had a special talent for castigating people in all tones of voice, from the obscene to the discreet, from the cruel to the caustic. His reproaches were like water dashed in our faces the whole day long. "Ignorant Annamese! Stupid Annamese!" or "Annamese are lazy. They steal all the time."[2] It was truly shameful, and deep inside we were livid with rage.

But anytime there was one among us who dared to raise a voice in protest, Father Quy would straightaway expel that student from the school. He was in a very strong position. Time and again he went to the district offices and the province chief's mansion. He would meet with the mandarins, both French and Vietnamese, until all hours of the night. Long afterwards, when I had been active in the revolution and had gained more experience, I realized that Father Quy's actions were those of a spy posing as a monk.

In 1926 there was in Vietnam a tumultuous struggle with the French imperialists, demanding that they free Phan Boi Chau.[3] Uncle Phan was a genuine and experienced patriot. He initiated the Dong Du movement, encouraging our youth to go abroad to study interesting professions and to gain new skills that might be of advantage to the country and of service to the people.

We loved to hear the stories of the young men who had fled to China and Japan. They were able to study at all the famous schools: the Japanese military academy; military engineering schools, technical schools; Whampoa, Tientsin, Tokyo, Wuhan. When we heard about it we were absolutely captivated. Vietnamese have been naturally inquisitive since ancient times. Besides, there was the burning urge to repay our debt to our country. Many of our youth thus listened to what Phan Boi Chau said and went to other countries. Wherever they studied, they sat in the first chair or the second chair. They had an upstanding attitude and bearing, so that no one could look on them as merely "exiles from an enslaved state."

Such tales spread from one mouth to another and finally reached us, exciting our patriotic spirit and arousing our pride in our people. Everyone now nurtured dreams of going abroad to learn a skill, then returning to help the country.

This really frightened the imperialists. They immediately colluded with the Chinese militarists to seize Uncle Phan by deception in the French Concession [in Shanghai] and return him to Vietnam. They plotted to bring him before a court, condemn him for some serious crime, and execute him. They originally intended to sentence Uncle Phan in a closed session, but people found out about it. At once, from south to north, letters asking for amnesty, petitions demanding release, flooded the offices of the French governor general and the resident superior of Tonkin.[4] They were forced to indict, try, and sentence Uncle Phan publicly, after which they detained him in Hue.

During that period Father Quy carried out a harsh investigation. He paid particular attention to people who were stubborn and wouldn't always do what he said. I was among the suspects. At Hoang Nguyen I had not been especially studious and was always practicing martial arts. On cool afternoons and moonlight nights I would invite several people who shared my ambitions out to the backyard of the seminary to practice with the fighting sticks. Father Quy wanted to forbid it, but did not have any pretext. We were only doing calisthenics, and what was wrong with that?

In fact, however, in the bottom of my heart I was thinking of learning the martial arts so that afterward I could help my country in the manner of De Tham and Phan Dinh Phung.[5] I had heard and read stories of the skills of the officers under the command of these men. Stories like these excited youth like me. Besides, I thought that practicing martial arts might prepare me to protect myself when I set out to study alone in some foreign land.

I continued to practice, and Father Quy continued to watch. He put my name down in his black book and waited for a chance to punish me. His habit of chewing us out grew worse every day. The students at the seminary were furious. Everyone was tired of living at Hoang Nguyen seminary.

Several months later there was a new movement in the country. One evening Hoang Nguyen received the news that Phan Chu Trinh was dead.[6] He was the man who had written a letter to King Khai Dinh recounting this scarecrow's antinational crimes when taking part in an exposition in France.[7] Phan Chu Trinh had also gone abroad to study new and interesting things to bring them back to help the country. We did not talk about the rights and wrongs of what he did.[8] At the time we simply knew that he was a patriot, so when we heard the news that he had passed away, our people deeply regretted it. Everywhere people met to hold ceremonies mourning him. From city to town, the news spread quickly throughout the whole country, and a movement to mourn Uncle Phan grew.

That movement sprang from the patriotic spirit of our people. Whenever it found a chance, a favorable occasion, that patriotic spirit flared up and spread everywhere. Thus, great numbers of people, even though they might not approve of the course Phan Chu Trinh had taken, took part in the struggle as a way of satisfying their patriotic urges.

At Hoang Nguyen seminary we also mourned Uncle Phan. I was the instigator and leader. Naturally Father Quy did not agree at all.

On the appointed day the students assembled on the seminary grounds, all wearing black mourning bands on their hats or their arms. Father Quy had given an order forbidding all this, but it was impossible to stop. He was so mad he was blue in the face. He stepped out on the veranda, called us to come close to him and roared out, "Annamese have no culture. Annamese are stupid and ignorant, ungrateful, don't even do what the people who teach them and care for them tell them to do."

I stood out in front of the line of people and replied, "Father, we have heard you teach that everyone is a child of God. And yet, Father, you curse Annamese as stupid, ignorant, ungrateful. We agree that Annamese are stupid, that Annamese are ignorant. But they make the rice that keeps people alive. And you, Father, eat this rice, too. When you berate us like this, doesn't it seem that you eat the fruit but don't remember who planted the tree? And when we mourn for a man of renown in our land like this, is it really reasonable to call us stupid, ignorant, and ungrateful?"

All around me the students gave their noisy support. Father Quy, half-angry and half-pale with shame, left immediately. Three days later he used his power as the head of Hoang Nguyen seminary to expel three students without giving a single reason. These three people he chose from those who, day after day, proved to be "hard-headed and stiff-necked"—who wouldn't do what he told them to. Naturally I was the first one he singled out.

Well, that was what constituted my crime of "troublemaking."

So I left Hoang Nguyen, supposing that I had escaped the burden of having to meet Father Quy every day of my life. But just think: if two streams run in opposite directions, they are bound to flow together eventually. In 1944 I again confronted Father Quy. By then our positions were conspicuously different. Father Quy was still Father Quy. He had the responsibility for baptizing and dispensing pardons to prisoners in the Hoa-lo jail in Ha-noi. Actually, however, he was there to seek out information for the French Secret Police. I was imprisoned there, but was no longer a naive youth just come of age. I had been forged by the party and by the revolution to become a person experienced in struggle.

When I met Father Quy I recognized him, but he did not recognize me. Thinking of how well I knew his private life, I asked my imprisoned comrades, "Would you like to have a good laugh?"

Everyone approved. I went out to meet Father Quy. This secret policeman in monk's garb missed no opportunity to propagandize and to introduce all manner of "spiritual medicine." He asked if I needed some books to read. I answered, "I really do, the more the better."

He gave me a stack of religious books. I took all of them so we could use the blank pages for preparing secret documents in the prison. Father Quy, feigning charity and righteousness, asked me, "What have you done, my child, that you must wear prison clothes? What is your crime?"

"I have committed no crime at all," I replied. "And you, Father, why must you wear that long coat?"

At my question the prisoners in the room burst out laughing because of a dirty joke, current at the time, about the long coat. Father Quy looked nonplussed. I asked another question: "Well, Father, have you brought any onions or garlic with you today?"

The prisoners again broke into laughter, but Father Quy completely missed the point of our mockery. Most days Father Quy brought along onions, garlic, and bread to try to win prisoners over. But when I asked my question, he did not suspect my double meaning, which used things he had taught me at the Hoang Nguyen school in years past. Now I was using his own lessons to flog him with. The Catholic religion has several commandments. The eighth one is: "You must not speak onions and garlic."[9] What it means is that a person should not spy on others or make up tales about them.

"Father, do you know why Jesus Christ was nailed to the cross?" I asked.

"Jesus Christ took upon himself the sins of the whole world," Father Quy replied.

"No," I laughed. "Jesus Christ campaigned among the Jewish people to rise up in revolution and strike down the Roman imperialists and Herod's gang of lackeys. He was defeated, they arrested him, and they executed him. That's all."

Father Quy evaded my gaze because he was afraid of my bringing out the truth like that.

That day we prisoners at Hoa-lo laughed until our sides hurt.

But that was much later. Back in 1926 Father Quy simply expelled me and my friends abruptly from Hoang Nguyen seminary.

～

At home they learned I had been expelled. My mother was very sad and disappointed. In a totally Catholic village life was very hard for a family that had a child expelled from the seminary or excommunicated for "rebelling against the will of God." Neighbors and relatives said one thing and another—all manner of reproaches. There was no lack of cruel words, insinuations, curses for the "atheist." For a woman like my mother, who had studied little and had been in the church since childhood, this grief was understandable. My mother's disappointment in me was even worse. My village was depressed and impoverished, with so little land in the communal fields that each time they were divided they averaged out to two and a half *sao* a person.[10] What little fruitful land existed was held by the village elders and notables. The poor were granted only plots which yielded dry or rotten harvests, where a year's work did not provide enough to pay the taxes. Yet who would not still hope that their children might eat? They grew what they could to take off some of the pressure.

My family was among the poorest in the village. My father made a living by collecting manure to sell to those families who had fields. All day long he wandered through the surrounding area, a pair of baskets on his shoulder, a picker in his hand. He returned home only after it was pitch-dark. Toiling as he did he still could not make enough to feed himself, to say nothing of raising us three children. Right up until the days before the August Revolution, my father had nothing to wear but his loincloth. There was not enough to eat, much less to send us children to school.

And yet my parents made every effort to send me to school, as if it were a matter of life and death. When I was still young, there was a traditional scholar named Le Huu Nhien who lived beside us and taught children the A-B-C's. Anxious to study, too, I usually hid in the courtyard to listen. Inside the house the scholar would teach a letter, and outside I would use a scrap of brick to write the letter on the ground. After a year of waiting, my mother finally found a bit of money and asked the scholar to let me enter the class. In four months I could read and write. My mother had found just enough money to pay the tuition; I had to manage the money for paper and pen on my own. In the mornings I went to school; then in the afternoon I took a basket and caught crabs to sell at the market. Besides that, during the fifth-month harvest I had to tend the teacher's buffalo, then cut grass for him and carry his child around. It was really a hardship for my parents to send me to school.

Thus, when I was accepted to study at the Hoang Nguyen seminary, my mother had great expectations. First, there would be one less mouth for the family to feed. More than that, she hoped I would pass the exams, get a position in the church, and begin to contribute some money to support the family. Then, suddenly, I was expelled. How do you suppose my mother felt? She yelled and screamed, giving me a very hard time. Even now I feel sorry for her when I think of it.

So far as I was concerned, though, being expelled from the Hoang Nguyen seminary did not leave me sad or disappointed. From the time I was still young, church dogma had gradually been losing its hold on me. When I was seven or eight and still in the village, I had to study the Bible. The teacher was a Mr. Trung. He would cane us terribly. I misbehaved a lot, so Mr. Trung really hated me and was always whipping me. Once he used a stiff rod to beat me until I was really sore. I was outraged, cursed back at him, and left the church for half a year. Mr. Trung sent some other children to catch me, intending to tie me up, bring me back, cane me and force me to fast. I picked up a knife and brandished it. The kids took to their heels. After that the priest had to call my mother to entice me back.

Another time my mother asked permission for me to study at the Trung-hieu parochial school. At that time labor was central to the curriculum in Trung-hieu parish. Besides saying prayers at mass and carrying candles, I had to cook, carry water, and do laundry, head bowed and eyes in the shadows the whole day long. When we studied, it was religious books in *nom*[11] and roman letters [*quoc ngu*].

At Trung-hieu parish there was an old teacher, Mr. San, who was the steward and kept the chest with all the keys. He was a good student of the scriptures and could say them from memory without the slightest hesitation. He was also a good drinker. Every night he would down bottle after bottle. San was a real woman chaser, too. The parish placed him in charge of hiring women to transplant rice and cut grass in the parish fields, so he hired them for the day's work and, when night came, seduced them outrageously. He used a rod to beat us. If we nodded off, we got a thrashing; didn't memorize the lesson, a thrashing; tardy or slow, a thrashing. He was addicted to beating. If he had a reason, he would beat us, and if he had no reason, he would beat us all the same. He made us bend over with our tails in the air and drop our pants. Then he used a rattan rod to whip us until we were sore. When he finished the beating, he made us eat only salted rice and sleep on the floor.

The life-styles of the various classes of people in the Trung-hieu parish house where we studied were clearly different. Thanks to offerings at mass and at prayers throughout the whole parish (which included six congregations from Ao-ca and Ao-cach to Kem-trong and So-kien), thanks to land rents, and thanks to money from lawsuits (the parish priest regularly interceded with district, prefecture, and province administrations, for a fee speaking on behalf of people who were bringing lawsuits), the priestly standard of living was quite high. They had three meals a day. At every meal the table was laden with braised pigeon, fried fish, and barbecued chicken. But month after month we students had nothing to eat but rice stretched with wormy corn and topped with spinach.

Studying did bring some bit of hope, though. Securing a position as priest was harder than getting to heaven. If that proved impossible, however, there was still the chance to become a teacher. This meant two meals of plain rice a day, a pile of rags to sleep on at night, and two suits of rough cloth supplied each year. It was a sad, lonely life. If you were sick, there was no one to care for you. I remember in those days there was one teacher who was ill for twelve days in a row, then died in a corner of his dark room. Yet no one knew, or at least they pretended not to know. They just brought him two bowlfuls of rice a day for form's sake. Twenty-four bowls of rice lined up at the foot of the wall. It was tragic and distressing. This was not something that could simply be dismissed as the man's fate.

∼

The things I witnessed at Tien-dong, at Trung-hieu, and at Hoang Nguyen caused me to lose all confidence in the justice of religion. And so, setting out from the Hoang Nguyen seminary I certainly did not feel the slightest grief or disappointment. But when I left the seminary at Hoang Nguyen I was truly at a loss, standing at a fork in the road. It was most important to choose the correct branch to follow. This choice could lead me to become a person useful to society, or it could lead me to a dead end, living in vain, dying pitifully.

It was a hard choice, and one I could not make right away. During the time I was searching for some direction, I resigned myself to seeking out some place to take refuge. If I went home, my family was too poor to support me. Actually, I could not have gone back even if I had wanted to. The village, including my family and friends, would have given me no peace. My hands knew no trade, and in my head there was only a pinch of *nom* and roman characters.[12] Where should I go? What should I do now? How could I make a living now? These were the questions that whirled through my head.

In the end I decided to go back to Vinh-tri and ask to live with Mr. Pho. Vinh-tri was a place I had once stayed to study Latin. Mr. Pho was a Vietnamese. He was very disgruntled because of the difference in treatment accorded to French and Vietnamese priests, so he incessantly took the French to task.

Precisely because of this difference in treatment, since 1919 a movement against foreign pastors had sprung up within the Vietnamese church to demand equality between French priests and Vietnamese priests. Mr. Pho was among those who shared this idea.

At Vinh-tri Mr. Pho gave me a job teaching the Bible, which I took to make a living. I would get two suits of clothing a year, and each month would receive sixty bowls of uncooked rice, two bottles of soy sauce, and a few cents with which to buy vegetables and incidentals. That was my life—wandering from village to village, a long road leading nowhere. Every day I had to teach Bible lessons which were no longer the least bit interesting to me. I had only a few good friends, one of them a young man who was a village teacher in Vinh-tri. I did not suspect that it was right here that I would find my way.

The teacher at Vinh-tri had many new magazines and books. Every time I went to visit him, I borrowed some of them to read. In those times village teachers were looked on as well-read, learned men. I very much liked to find them, to visit with them and talk. I had to do it secretly because the church forbade keeping company with people who read modern literature.

The teacher at Vinh-tri confided many things to me about the hard life of the people of the area, who tried to make a living by making pictures and rosaries for the mission. I, too, spoke of my personal feelings. It was precious indeed to meet another patriot and to be able to reveal thoughts that normally had to be hidden deep in my heart. I told him about the life at the seminary and the things I had found out there. I had the prayers down pat, but they did not stir my spirit in the least. The stories that I liked and absorbed, which came together for me when I heard them explained at the school, were the historical tales about ancient heroes. Little David, the poor shepherd who dared to stand up for his people and his fatherland, to face the enemy general, the fierce giant Goliath. I was very fond of the image of the little boy going into battle with his sling, daring to fight and defeat Goliath. Or there was the story of the heroine Joan of Arc, the French shepherd girl who led her people in a struggle to preserve her motherland. When she was captured by the enemy, she was burned to death on a pyre. Besides these, there were courageous examples I could read surreptitiously in the modern literature. The person I admired most was De Tham, the tiger of Yen-the region, who opposed the French continually for dozens of years until his death, and never submitted.

The teacher at Vinh-tri recounted my confidences to another person, a man who was to open for me a path which moves me every time I think of it. That was Tong Van Tran.[13] I was able to meet Tran twice in the North, two meetings I shall never forget so long as I live.

Sometime about May 1927 I was teaching Bible classes in Phong-doanh District (now Y-yen District in Nam-dinh Province). One day in May, at noontime, I was going along a dike in the hot, blinding sun on the way to a village to teach Bible classes. The fields on both sides of the road were filled with ripe, golden rice. Beautiful as the scene was, I could only ponder the strange dead-end situation I was in. Suddenly from off in the distance someone came riding a bicycle toward me, heading in the opposite direction. He was wearing a long white gown and a white hat, and had Bata[14] shoes on. When he drew close, he got off his bicycle and greeted me.

I had never met him before, but the man had a special air that arrested my attention immediately. This was Tran. He was tall and slender, with a bright shining face. His head was large, and his jaw jutted out a bit. He had a broad, high forehead, stubborn and determined. He spoke with a resonant voice that sounded happy and absolutely open. He had the appearance of a courageous hero. He introduced himself and said to me, "When I heard about you, I wanted to meet you so we could talk."

So the two of us walked along side by side on the dike, following the Vinh-tri River, talking frankly for hours. "So what are you doing for a living now?" Tran asked me.

I do not know why it was that after only a few minutes of conversation I felt an immediate fondness for him—had confidence in him at once. I revealed all my feelings to Tran without hesitation. Then he asked me, "What do you think about the future, about our country?"

I told him all about the impasse I faced, my lack of direction. Right away Tran told me about Phan Boi Chau and Phan Chu Trinh. When I heard him, I had a premonition of the sort of person I had met. And then he talked to me about a secret society—a secret society I had heard of since 1925 or 1926, which the people in charge of the Hoang Nguyen seminary like Father Quy denounced as pagan. But when Tran talked about the secret society that day it seemed like just what my heart—craving some way to save the country—needed. I was intoxicated by his account.

After several hours of conversation while we walked along the dike, Tran bade me farewell and promised to meet me again at his house. Before we parted, Tran warned me to keep everything secret and not to let anyone know we had met. He had one more thing to say in lieu of a farewell: "We young people must be of one heart to save the country."

I had found my way. At the time I thought that surely Tran was in the secret society. If I followed him, I would find the way to save our country. I would be able to go abroad to study, then come back to help the nation. The only thing that puzzled me was how he knew about me. It was only long afterwards that I realized the teacher at Vinh-tri had introduced me to Tran.

The night after the meeting with Tran I tossed and turned and couldn't get to sleep. I was anxious to meet him again and hear him talk. So I was right on time when the appointed day arrived. This second meeting was at his house in a village not far away.

This time Tran carefully told me many things about a faraway land where the workers and peasants had seized power and were controlling their own destiny. That was the Soviet Union. He told me that he was a member of the Viet Nam Revolutionary Youth League.[15] He advised me to study hard so I could be accepted as a league member.

I declared my intention to study abroad. "If you go to the South, it will be easy to go abroad and study," Tran replied. "But the purpose of overseas study is to save the country—to make revolution. And if you want to make a revolution to strike down the French, you must depend on the workers and peasants at home. If you want to regain national independence, then you must strike down the imperialists. If you want to secure land for the impoverished tillers, then you must strike down the feudal landlords."

"If you want the workers to trust you, so that you can make a revolution together," he advised me, "you must proletarianize yourself."

I was at a loss, and asked, "How do I proletarianize myself?"

"You must frequent places where workers are—like ports, factories, rubber plantations," Tran explained. "The goods of this life are all created by their hands, and they will control the destiny of humanity. You must go in and live among them, campaign with them and learn from them in order to make the revolution together. Only then can you succeed."

These two meetings with brother Tran were only a few hours long, but they had unraveled a knot for me, one which I had been unable to unravel for myself in several years of trying. Unfortunately for me, Tran had to leave Vinh-tri for Hai-phong after that and did not have time to tell me good-bye. He had come unexpectedly and then departed unexpectedly, leaving me with so much regret in my heart, at a loss, with no one to show me the way.

Afterwards I met Tran one last time. At that time I was a Communist party member being deported to Con-son Island by the French imperialists. The ship taking us past Cap Saint Jacques (Vung Tau) in the South met the ship *Claude Chappe*, which was also delivering political prisoners from the North to Con-son. Standing at the side of the ship and looking through a crack in the hatch, I felt a warm rush of joy when I saw that the prisoners on the *Claude Chappe* had proudly unfurled a deep red hammer and sickle flag right on the enemy ship. The prisoners from the *Claude Chappe* were brought over to our ship for the journey out to Con-son. At once I went to meet the person who had unfurled that hammer and sickle flag, intending to express my admiration. Who do you suppose it turned out to be but my old friend Tong Van Tran!

The two earlier meetings with Tran, brief as they were, had increased my resolution and increased my confidence in the course I had just discovered: the road of proletarianized revolutionary struggle. Since Tran had left Vinh-tri so abruptly, I had not yet had the honor of standing in the ranks of the Viet Nam Revolutionary Youth League, but I could never forget his advice. I was determined to do as he had said.

~

In the middle of 1927 the French imperialists were doing all they could systematically to take advantage of our people, through their

Second Indochina Exploitation Plan. Many factories and plantations sprang up. Projects in construction, highways, bridges, and locks developed rapidly. All the capital, talent, and materiel that were flung into this period of exploitation had been drawn from the blood and bones of our people. A great deal of land was taken over. Plantations like the one at Chi-ne took thousands of hectares of the people's land. Who knows how many cruel and senseless taxes were proclaimed and dumped on the heads and shoulders of our already impoverished people, making them poorer still.

At every intersection, on all the market stalls, advertising posters were pasted up to recruit workers to go to the New Hebrides, to go South, to work in the mines and on the plantations.

The French colonialists had a shortage of workers for their plan of exploitation, so the advertisements were overflowing with words of sugar and honey. They said workers would go for a period of three years, and at the end of that period they could return home with all their transportation expenses paid; that there would be three square meals a day, with beef and fish; that there would be seven kilograms of rice a month, and two suits of work clothes a year; that in case of illness workers would be cared for and would not have to pay for their medicines; that before they left each person would receive ten piasters to pay for their immediate needs; and so on.

When they were unable to recruit enough labor, the French colonialists threw in Vietnamese contractors to coax and con farmers in the Red River delta who had lost their land and were down on their luck with no opportunity to escape their lot. There was an abundance of recruiting activity everywhere. The contracting gangs tried to outdo each other in spinning fantastic images of the out-of-this-world way of life on the rubber plantations, because they received two piasters for each person they handed over to the French.

I was not deceived by their honeyed words and their suave advertising. I knew that to go meant suffering and danger—that you might go but you could not be sure of returning. But if I stayed where I was, I would die, too. I had no trade, no place to stay, not even a garden to plant. If I did not find some way to make a living, a revolutionary road, then there was no other way. My road to the rubber plantation had already been determined. Only by entering upon it would I be able to accomplish my goal of proletarianizing myself so I could work for the revolution.

And so, along with hundreds of other people from Ha-nam, Nam-dinh, and Ninh-binh provinces, I signed my name at a recruiting office to go work on a rubber plantation in the South. Thus began a phase of my life which would make me comprehend fully what revolution was and give me a deep understanding of the workers, the leading class of revolution in this era.

THE ROAD INTO HELL

People often say that rubber workers have a spirit of determination, even of life-or-death struggle, and will never retreat. And they are not mistaken, because not only were rubber workers exploited and repressed in the extreme on the rubber plantations, but they were even exploited and repressed while they were on the road to those hells on earth.

In June 1927 we newly recruited workers had been gathered by the hundreds and crammed into the recruiting service's bamboo and thatch camps at Ha-ly and Hai-phong.

It was heartrending to see the recruited workers awaiting the ships. We were all farm folk from the provinces of Ha-nam, Nam-dinh, Thai-binh, and Ninh-binh. We did not have an inch of land, nor even one zinc coin. These were people forced by intolerable circumstances to band together and go to work the rubber plantations; few were actually taken in by the enticing words of the recruiters.

Only after they left their home villages did they come to know each other. For ages farming folk had seldom paid any attention to events beyond the bamboo hedges of our own villages. People usually had to work night and day just to survive. The spring harvest was hardly over when it was time to work on the fall crop. When the fertilizing was done, it was time to cultivate the corn and yams. When did we have any time to think of more distant matters?

And yet, as soon as we left our home villages, we were living together and protecting each other. There was one very intense thing that drew us into a tightly knit group. At the time we did not recognize it. It was only much later that we understood it: that people in a common situation of poverty, of oppression, must unite, must join together in order to have any hope of securing a morsel of food or a scrap of clothing.

We had to stay at Ha-ly to wait for the ship. Hundreds of people divided up the living space in rows of steel-roofed sheds, broad as an elephant cage, but squat and unbearably hot. On all four sides was a swamp of stinking sewage. The people from Thai-binh were in one section, then those from Ha-nam, from Ninh-binh—each province to its own section. I lived with the natives of Ha-nam. They were fond of me because I was very direct and because I took care of the sick and the exhausted. Besides, I knew how to write, and I often helped them with letters—a few lines to send back to their loved ones before they set out.

This was one reason that during the struggle of the people from Nam-dinh and Thai-binh, the recruit workers from Ha-nam listened to me and supported them wholeheartedly, even though they were hardly involved in the affair at all.

That incident set the whole port in an uproar. When we left home and came to Ha-ly, we had all signed contracts with the contracting foremen. This bunch were the right-hand men of the recruiters. Two clauses of the contracts were involved in the struggle at Ha-ly. One said that the contracting foreman had to provide food and water for the recruits: two *xu* per meal per person.[1] If they had spent the proper amount of money, it would still have been necessary to supplement the rations. But at the time the contractors were only providing 1.2 *xu*. The rice was rotten, and when it was scooped out of the pot it stank like roach dung and stuck together in chunks. The dried fish was completely rotten, and no matter how much salt they added in the kitchen, the stench was still unbearable. When this situation was discovered, the recruits from those provinces all raised a furious storm of protest.

There was another clause which was not written down in the contracts—something the recruiters said to entice the poor to sign on as laborers. They said that they would give each worker ten *dong* to take care of various miscellaneous expenses before leaving. The contractors raked off part of that from the very first. In the case of the brothers and sisters from Ha-nam, including me, they had said ten *dong* all along, so we all got the full amount. But in the case of the brothers and sisters from Nam-dinh and Thai-binh, they gave each person only six *dong*.

How could our country folk, who always were so trusting, be aware of such mean maneuvers? Actually, they could not even read the provisions of the contracts they had signed. And there were some who were tricked into signing the contracts like this: The recruiters said they had to take the workers' pictures to give to the government. Then, if anything happened later, the government would come to their aid. So they took each laborer off to have his picture made. They took profiles; they took full-face shots—all kinds. After that, they held out a piece of paper and told the person to make his mark so he could get the pictures later. Only afterwards did the workers learn that the piece of paper was in fact a preprinted contract. The person who had been thus deceived did not realize that he was putting his mark to a piece of paper in which he sold his life and his freedom to a capitalist master.

When the workers did not even know what was in the written contracts they had signed, naturally no one bothered to tell them what the "verbal understandings" were. The contractors, "working on a case-by-case basis," would skim a few *dong* from this person and a few *dong* from the next.

So the brothers and sisters from Nam-dinh and Thai-binh who received six *dong* each were content to have received that much. But when a man keeps stuffing gold into his pocket, it will eventually show. When they got to Ha-ly one person asked another, and the recruits from Nam-dinh and Thai-binh were shocked when they found out that the contractors had skimmed off four dong from them.

The brothers from Ha-nam came to discuss the matter of the money rake-off with me. I answered, "We are all in the same situation. If they ask us, we ought to go along and lend them a hand." And then, with everyone enraged by the miserable food, the struggle broke out. It was a struggle, but the truth was there was no leadership committee and there was no organized rank and file. It was simply a spontaneous struggle by people who had reached the end of their rope, who no longer knew what fear was. My role was only that of spokesman.

Our adversary in the struggle at that time was Phan Tat Tao. This character was a contractor who, along with the recruiters, had stepped forward to lure people from northern Viet Nam and sell them to the French. Tao very seldom came to the section of Ha-ly where the sheds were. He normally just let his henchmen deal with the recruits. And he was never present at our meals.

That noon, as at every meal, each person got only one bowl of rice with a piece of dried fish the size of three fingers. As usual it was heavily salted fish—putrid and stinking. The bucket of tea, too, had just enough for each person to have one bowlful. And so it was that the struggle broke out. We refused to eat. Hundreds of voices shouted out for Phan Tat Tao to come. Tao's henchmen were scared out of their wits. When they saw us shouting and going on a hunger strike, they cleared out.

Our shouts rocked the whole Ha-ly area. At the time we did not realize that the struggle had broken out at a particularly opportune moment. The colonialists needed many more sites as way stations for the recruit workers. While they remained on northern soil, near their home villages, it was quite easy for recruits to desert and return home in waves. So Phan Tat Tao had to come and talk to us. At first he tried to smooth things over with us, saying he would see to it that our food was improved. But we protested noisily, demanding that Tao carry out his promises, that he implement all provisions of the contract. The workers said, "We have sold our homes, sold our lives for ten dong, and if you don't pay it all, we aren't leaving."

Phan Tat Tao saw we were tense, saw from our attitude and words that we were quite determined. He knew things were going badly and that he would have to give in to us. That very noon meal he prepared extra rations. As for the money that had been raked off from the brothers and sisters from Thai-binh and Nam-dinh, he was so ashamed that that very night he had his henchmen bring the money, call out names, and place the proper amount in each person's hand.

So our first struggle was victorious. This experience showed me all the more clearly that, although peasants usually kept things to themselves, whenever they were thrown together they were very much in sympathy with each other.

The struggle had just ended. While I was staying at Hai-phong, I was able to meet brother Tong Van Tran again. Tran was very glad to hear the news of our victory. He both praised me and admonished me: "That's the way! Just be sure to keep it up now." His admonition was engraved deeply in my heart. Afterwards we always stayed on the offensive against the enemy, thanks to that precious advice.

And then the ship which was to take us away docked in Hai-phong. The *Commandant Dorier* was a cargo ship which often docked at Hai-phong to take on Thai-nguyen iron ore to carry to France. This time, besides a quantity of ore, there was a cargo of people—us.

When we boarded the ship we recruit workers divided up the spaces according to provinces of origin, Ha-nam in one area, then Nam-dinh and Thai-binh, each province with its own section. The ship's master tossed each person a sleeping mat to spread out right on the deck of the ship. This was used as both sleeping and eating space.

After our successful struggle, our spirits were high and the bonds of mutual sympathy were very strong. A small number who had been indifferent before, including even village notables who had lost their money, lost their jobs, and left home to find work, were now drawn along, too. A number of Ha-nam youth of around my age admired my spirit of daring to act and to take on hardship. They drew along with them a number of youth from Nam-dinh and Thai-binh as well. It would have been natural for that camaraderie to have mellowed our anxiety as we set out for a distant land to seek our livelihood. But the situation forced us to launch a new struggle.

The captain of the *Dorier* was a French lieutenant-commander. All the sailors were French, too. The ship's galley did not give us enough to eat. The food was as miserable as what we had been given at Ha-ly. We had gained experience in struggle from the Phan Tat Tao affair. Everyone protested noisily and sought me out to ask my opinion. I discussed the situation with each person, and in the end all were united in the opinion that we must struggle.

I agreed to step forward to talk with the ship's master. At the time some of the brothers on the ship had passed their certificate exams,[2] and could speak French fairly well. I gathered nine or ten of them together. I thought we might need someone to take my place if the situation got tense and the ship's master took me away. That possibility forced me to seek out more supporters.

At noon we went on a hunger strike and asked for the ship's master. In a moment the lieutenant-commander who was captain of the ship came into the hold. I stepped forward and spoke to him in French on behalf of the brothers and sisters.

"According to our contracts, we are supposed to have enough to eat, meat with our rice, and hot tea to drink. But the galley doesn't give us enough to eat, and there's not enough to drink, either. We ask that you carry out the contract."

The ship's master flushed with anger. "If I let you eat your fill and you get seasick and vomit it up all over the deck, what then?" he retorted.

I did not accept that, and responded, "What you say is not right. We have a right to eat our fill. When we've eaten our fill there may be some who will vomit and others who won't. But you must let us eat our fill."

The ship's master would not debate the matter further and abandoned reason entirely. He exploded in a rage, treacherously seized me and threatened to throw me into the sea. I was not frightened by his threats and held fast to the opinion I had expressed. After that, he shut me up in the toilet and told everyone they had to eat what they were given. He was not prepared for our spirit of solidarity and determination. As much as he threatened the brothers and sisters, they were still determined to live or die together and refused to eat. The French sailors admired us. They tossed the recruits packets of bread and cheese. They winked and waved and signaled to encourage us to keep it up.

By that evening the ship's master had to compromise and give us decent food. That meal we even had beef. And the master released me. The recruit workers were elated and gave me a cordial welcome.

So the group of converts to my cause had grown much larger than the original handful of youth. At that time, just eighteen, I was rather nice looking, upstanding, and unpretentious by nature, and easily won the affections of all. My name at that time was Pham Van Phu. The recruits held me in esteem and called me "young uncle." They had absolute confidence in "uncle" Phu, and came to ask me about everything.

The French sailors also liked me. The very day of my victorious struggle, they sought me out; took me back to their quarters; and brought out wine, bread, and beef for a party. We laughed and joked together. And after that we sang French and Vietnamese folk songs for each other.

After that struggle, I became the ad hoc representative for our group of recruits. When anything came up, they sought me out to ask me or tell me about it. The same thing went for the master and his gang. Whenever he wanted to communicate anything to the recruits, the ship's master would come looking for me. But these relatively comfortable circumstances only lasted for a short time, during the final days on the *Dorier*. When we reached Khanh-hoi (in Sai-gon), the cruel and repressive nature of the rubber plantation owners became very apparent.

As soon as the *Dorier* docked in Sai-gon, the overseers, both French and Vietnamese, sprang noisily aboard. They used canes on the heads of the recruits, counting us like animals. Our baggage—simple bags and baskets—was scattered and torn, and some people's wives and children got tangled up in their loads. The whole throng—hundreds of people—was driven ashore by the overseers like a herd of cattle.

On the shore the police swarmed like flies. They divided up and stood on both sides of the street, one every ten meters, bull-dicks (rawhide blackjacks) and billy clubs ready in their hands. Meanest of all were the half-breeds. They constantly cursed: "You mother fuckers! Savages!" As they cursed, they flailed about with their clubs, aiming at our heads and necks. And the others were no laggards. They constantly urged us on with: "Move it on, move it on," at the same time lashing out with their clubs. The brothers and sisters were seething with rage, but because there had been no advance preparations to deal with this situation, we had to restrain ourselves and go on to the assembly area.

When we reached the place, as soon as they had set down their crumpled parcels they came to see me. We discussed the situation among ourselves and selected a representative to intercede with the overseers. I was not the one to step forward this time. The task of representing us was given to a man named Truong Lap. Brother Lap was originally from Cat-lai in Binh-luc District. He was tall and strong, and his face was always red as a beet. He was bold by nature and refused to retreat no matter what the difficulty. Whatever danger he encountered, he was unwavering and had a spirit as hot as a cobra.

We shouted out, demanding to meet with the chief recruiter to protest the beatings. The overseers and police closed in. "What's all this shouting about?" one of them asked us.

"Masters, you have cursed and beat us from the side of the ship all the way up here," Lap exploded provocatively. "Now what if I curse you once and see what you think about it?" The overseers and police moved in at once and beat us unmercifully. They bashed brother Truong Lap on the head with a billy club and laid him out on the ground, blood streaming out all over his body. I cried out to the brothers. They began to shout and went on a rampage. This frightened the overseers and police, and they ran out to call the Secret Police inspector. A short while later, they swarmed in like bees. The man in the lead was a Frenchman who spoke Vietnamese quite well. "What's going on?" he asked. "What do you little ones think you are doing?"

Angry because they were treating us like animals, and madder still because this Frenchman was addressing us like children, I boiled over and stepped forward to answer: "We 'gentlemen' signed a contract to come down here to work. The contract promised there would be no beatings. Yet they have beaten us 'men.' That is not lawful. If they continue to beat us, we 'men' will take them to court!"

On all sides the brothers shouted out curses. Seeing the situation was tense, the inspector backed down. "Come on, 'kids,' keep it orderly and there won't be any problem."

He was afraid the sound of the shouting would be heard beyond the compound, and he wanted to finish transferring the workers to the rubber company so he would no longer be responsible. He agreed to transfer the two half-breed overseers who had beaten us most harshly. And he allowed Lap to be taken to the hospital for treatment. Brother Lap died later at Phu-rieng in 1928. If he had not died, he would surely have turned into a fine fighter.

After this skirmish, we finally took a look at our new quarters, which the overseers called the arrival department. In fact, this arrival department was a branch of the inspectorate for southern Viet Nam. It was exactly like a concentration camp, with barbed wire fences on all four sides and gendarmes and police inspectors standing guard day and night. Inside were rows of steel-roofed barracks. Each barracks had two rows of ironwood pilings, one on either side. Inside the barracks it was pitch-dark since there was not so much as a single window—only the big door where people went in and out.

The inspectors carried out constant searches. Those who had not yet signed contracts were forced to complete everything. The contract had several conditions which were quite seductive, but which were never carried out. It also had many provisions which were very severe. According to the contract, rubber workers would have their wages computed daily, would have living quarters provided, would have a clinic providing free medical treatment, and could purchase food at low plantation rates. At the end of the three-year contract, they would be able to return to their home villages, and the plantation owner would bear all expenses of the return journey.

In any event, none of the above provisions were carried out, or if they were, they were not carried out fully. For example, speaking of free medical care I will simply mention that whenever someone was sick and went up to the plantation clinic to ask for medicine, the plantation nurses would give him a very "efficient" kind of treatment—telling him to fast for a few days to halt the "progress" of the disease. So the sick person would not dare go for an examination after that, no matter how severe his illness. Or there were many conditions we had to force them to implement, like the clause on hot tea for us to drink during working hours.

And there were a great many of the harsh clauses. One of them provided that anyone who did not follow orders from a superior, who was disruptive, caused an incident, or was absent without permission would be fined. On the second offense he would be imprisoned for five to ten days in solitary confinement if the offense was termed "disturbing the peace."

Another provision said: Women shall not be given work beyond their strength; a woman shall be entitled to one month's maternity leave before she bears her child, and for two months after she gives birth she shall only be assigned light work. But in reality the women had to endure a more shameful situation than the men. I will recount those episodes later.

At the Khanh-hoi arrival service it was about a week before all the paperwork was finished. During the time we were waiting, we grew closer and closer to each other. When we talked, it was entirely about practical matters. For instance we said, "We have come here, far from our villages, far from our homes, and we have no close relatives. So we must learn to protect each other." Or, "They bristle with guns and clubs. We will have to unite our forces if we want to survive." Or, "Let's try to take care of each other, wait until the end of the three-year contract, then go back to our families, our villages, and our home region." But, in fact, very few would be able to go home.

One day trucks from the rubber companies pulled up at the arrival center. At that time there were many large companies in the rubber sector in southern Viet Nam, such as the Compagnie des Terres Rouges. The reason it had this name was that in the south there were two kinds of soil suitable for growing rubber, one red and the other gray. Besides the Compagnie des Terres Rouges there were Mimot, Michelin, and the "Tropic Tree" company. Each established a number of different plantations. They divided the land among themselves to plunder it. Companies applied to open up as much as 50,000 hectares at a time. So they were very short of labor. Every time new recruit workers arrived, they had to be divided among the various companies to see to it that each company received a fair share.

So it was this time, too. They divided us up to go to rubber plantations at Sa-cam, Sa-cat, Loc-ninh, Dau-tieng, Bo-dot, and Phu-rieng. They divided us up according to our native provinces. So a hundred and fifty from Ha-nam, including me, were taken to Phu-rieng. The Phu-rieng group was taken off last of all.

I do not have to tell you how upset we were at being divided up into six or seven groups like that. We had come to feel very close after those days of hunger, ill-treatment, whippings, and victorious struggle so far from home. We had felt certain we would live or die together for the next three years. So you can ask yourself how heartsick we felt at having to part overnight like that.

In my own case, the brothers and sisters from Thai-binh and Nam-dinh and I felt very attached to each other. They bid me a reluctant farewell, took their things, and boarded the truck. "If only you could go with me, Uncle, it would be so good," someone said to me. I was very moved and very sad when I saw their affection and their confidence in me. I could think of nothing to say except to admonish them, "Go on, now. I hope you'll stick together and return home after three years. Maybe we'll be able to go back on the same ship."

At that time we did not imagine that the number of people who would escape death would be so small. Nor could we imagine the kind of lives we would lead at the rubber plantations. It is fortunate that someone lived through it all to recount the horrible scenes of those hells on earth.

All the other groups left the arrival department one after another. The hundred and fifty of us from Ha-nam set out in the last load, bound for Phu-rieng. I stayed there three years, but at the end of my term instead of being able to return home I was taken out on a ship to Con-son by the imperialists.

But that story comes three years later.

HELL ON EARTH

After a bone-jarring, soul-shattering two-day truck ride, a hundred and fifty of us from Ha-nam set foot on Phu-rieng soil. As we stepped down from the truck, each of us looked apprehensively at the place that would be our home for three years.

Phu-rieng lies at the extreme west of the Di-linh high plateau. It is about two or three hundred meters above sea level, with six- and seven-hundred-meter high hills scattered all around. Phu-rieng lies in the heart of an ancient tropical forest. To the north is a border area where southern and central Viet Nam meet Cambodia. To the west is the Loc-ninh forest area, and then modern day Kampuchea. The forests here were in their natural state, never yet exploited by the hand of man. The rouge red soil was extremely fertile. It was originally jet black rock rained down by volcanic eruptions, broken down over the ages into fertile earth. So bamboo stalks sprouted one on top of the other. The trees were so huge that it took seven or eight people to reach completely around one. The oil trees and hardwoods rose high overhead, spreading the shade of their overlapping branches so that even the rays of the noonday sun could not penetrate.

We ragged and forlorn lowlanders were completely staggered by that extraordinary scene. It made each of us all the more worried and homesick.

The Phu-rieng plantation was part of the property of the Michelin rubber company. We were the first group of workers to arrive to clear the land. It was a vast plantation, about twenty kilometers long and more than ten kilometers wide. They had set up a village about every kilometer. Since we were the first group of workers, we lived in village number one. In each village the plantation built rows of barracks. Each barracks provided living quarters for fifty workers. Inside the barracks they had set up wooden partitions dividing them up into ten sections. Each section was a square five meters on a side. We divided ourselves up five people to a section. We slept right on the long wooden floor and cooked in our own section. The sections were so crowded that we got to our feet only when we went in and out. The sanitary conditions were also extremely poor.

On rainy days it flooded, and when the sun shone it was scorching. The climate in the region was oppressively hot and humid, but there were no windows in the barracks. And they had low steel roofs. We felt that we were living in ovens the whole year round.

In terms of organization, each village was both a production unit and an administrative unit. When the siren sounded for work, we divided into teams of about ten, with a Vietnamese foreman to watch us. Above the foremen were the overseers, each of whom watched several teams. They were generally half-French. These overseers were in turn under the authority of a number of chief overseers. They were the ones who directed all operations at Phu-rieng.

Each had their special rights and privileges. The Vietnamese foremen did not get so very much more than we did. There was just the slightest difference between their pay and ours, but they had individual living compartments. From the overseers on up, however, life was completely different from ours. Each overseer had two spacious rooms, high and dry, and fully equipped with table and chairs, bed and cabinets, and all manner of pots and pans. The chief overseers had their own private houses in each village. Each house was well ventilated, with proper glass windows and shutters. Inside, it was divided into four clean, well-kept rooms: two bedrooms, a dining room, and a room for receiving visitors. The furniture was beautifully made of fine wood, the veneer polished until it shone. Workers very seldom set foot in the chief overseer's house except when he called them up to question them about something. And the chief overseer had the right to bring a number of workers to his house to cook for him, clean and dust the house, or do his laundry.

Above them all was the manager. He was like the prince of the plantation. He had an elegant house in bungalow style. He also had several private cars—one he might use around the plantation, another to go off on trips, yet another for the family to use when they went out on pleasure drives. In the bungalow there were always dozens of servants, from secretaries, drivers, "boys," and cooks to servant girls and gardeners. The manager's house was off limits like the private chambers of a king or a prince. No worker dared to come close. I lived there three years, but only set foot in the manager's house once, when Phu-rieng exploded into struggle in 1930, and we took over the plantation for several days.

This whole crew, from the manager to the overseers, was recruited from the French army. I will describe and name some of the most "famous" later. In general they were executioners—the terrible, cruel demons of this hell on earth, Phu-rieng. Whoever cursed the workers well would be quick to get a raise. Whoever beat workers with true cruelty would get a raise especially fast.

The most common forms of punishment were to make the person drop his pants, then beat him on the buttocks, or beat his feet until the soles were in ribbons. After a beating, the worker would be locked up in a dark room, legs shackled, and left without food for two or three days. Some people were forgotten there until they died of thirst.

Women workers who were the least bit attractive were even more to be pitied. The chief overseer and the ordinary overseers, then the French foremen and the Vietnamese foremen, would call them up. After only a few weeks their bodies had faded like fallen leaves. And if the woman was married, her husband would be involved, too. Anyone who resisted what was happening would be beaten to death. The poor husband would be robbed of his wife until—by the time they had crushed her and grown tired of her, then let her go—he had died of humiliation and heartbreak.

The very day after we arrived at Phu-rieng, the masters passed out the tools of our trade. Each person received a palm leaf hat and a poncho; each person had to keep and care for a pruning hook, a hoe, and an ax. The tools were all of good quality steel imported from France. We had to keep them shining and sharp. The overseers constantly inspected them, and any time they saw one a bit dull or with even a hint of rust, it would be cause for a painful blow. Besides those items, each person was issued a numbered piece of wood to hang around his neck like a prison number.

At that time Phu-rieng was still a tropical rain forest without a single rubber tree. We had to clear each section of forest to prepare it for planting the rubber trees. The early days of the clearing effort were especially hard and dangerous, but we had no assistance at all. First of all, we workers had to fell the trees, clear out the underbrush, dry everything in the sun, and then burn it. It was extremely hazardous work, felling those giant hardwoods and oil trees, which had branches reaching out who knows how far above. Each time a tree was felled and came crashing down, the rushing sound of the branches lashing the air was terrifying to hear. After the crash of each tree, the workers held their breath and listened to see if anyone was crying out. On some days two or three people were crushed by trees. There would be at least several people with legs broken, arms put out of joint, or faces slashed as the small branches whipped by. As evening grew closer and more trees fell, people grew more tired, no longer so quick on their feet as in the early morning. That was when the most accidents occurred.

When we were felling trees there were few weeks when no one was crushed to death by a tree. As we went to work each morning we were anxious, not knowing whether when evening came we would still be alive to return. The work was extremely arduous as well.

Every morning we had to get up at four o'clock to cook our food. At five-thirty we all had to form ranks in the village courtyard so the overseers could check the roll. As they did this, some of the overseers would use their batons, whacking the workers' heads as they counted them. There was not one of them who did not play that game. There was another game, however, in which they took particular delight. Whenever anyone was a few minutes late, they would fine him one *dong*, though our pay at the time was only four *hao*[1] per workday.

After roll call, the overseers took us out to the work area from six in the morning until six in the evening. We had to toil steadily under the sun, hot as fire, except for fifteen minutes at noon to eat, drink, and relieve ourselves.

The overseers drove us to fell trees, clear out underbrush, then dig holes to plant the rubber trees without rest. Finally at six in the evening we returned to the village, everyone of us bone tired. But when we reached the village, we had to busy ourselves carrying bamboo tubes down to the stream for water, and finding a few sticks of dry firewood to kindle a fire to cook our dinner. We would then grill our dried fish on the fire until we could smell it charring, then toss everything together and eat. When we were especially dried out, we might go hunt for mushrooms and leaves like poor scholars, cooking some tasteless soup of mangosteen leaves or whatever we happened to find to ease the pain.

At the end of the day a person really had no enthusiasm left, but wanted nothing more than to slip into the barracks and fall asleep so that the next day, when the overseer's siren sounded again, he could get up, eat, and begin another day of backbreaking work. One's strength today was never what it had been the day before. Every day one was worn down a bit more, cheeks sunken, teeth gone crooked, eyes hollow with dark circles around them, clothes hanging from collarbones. Everyone appeared almost dead, and in fact in the end about all did die.

The forest was filled with mosquitoes, every one of them enormous and bright orange with glistening wings. They came buzzing through the air, then lighted and bit right through our clothes. These were malarial mosquitoes, and when they landed on us they arched their backs into the air. Even so, drinking water was not boiled. Whoever was thirsty just searched for some crevice or hole in the ground to drink from. So malaria spread among us extremely quickly. Within a month after we arrived at Phu-rieng there was not one among us who had not been stricken with the fever.

Besides the mosquitoes there were the ox-flies, round as castor beans and purplish red. Wherever they bit, they left gaping wounds which quickly grew deeper and wider. If the infection was not stopped, it would cripple a person.

But the mosquitoes and ox-flies of Phu-rieng were not so fearsome as the army ants. In this red-earth high plateau there were more of these ants than the ordinary type. About four in the afternoon, long lines of them would move out, small worker ants in the middle, fighting ants with heads twice as large as their bodies, mandibles like the claws of a crab, positioned on both flanks as guards. Whenever they reached a field, the whole column of ants would stop, the fighters would turn their heads to face outwards all around, stretch their necks, display their mandibles, and tramp noisily on dry leaves.

This strain of ants had bodies as big as the joint of a man's finger. If we walked over them on our way to a work site, their two mandibles would snap together on our flesh, drawing blood. In a person's flesh the two pincers would lock tightly together so that when the creature was pulled off, only the body would come. The head would break off, leaving the pincers fastened deep in the person's flesh. There were some among us who knew nothing of this strain of ants at first. One day a fellow native of Ha-nam was so exhausted from work that he had a fever and could not stand up. He had to lie down right at the work site. That night, the jungle ants came out to feed. By morning there was nothing left of this unfortunate fellow but a stark white skeleton. So those evenings when we were late returning from work, the sound of army ants feeding raised goose flesh on us all.

Although we worked unbearably hard in a region with an inhospitable climate, we still had to endure an extremely austere diet. According to the contract which we had signed earlier, we were to be given rice at no charge, and should have been able to buy other food inexpensively from the plantation. But now we had to accept a deduction for twenty-four pounds of rice from each month's salary. And no one was allowed to buy rice or other foodstuffs from the outside as they wished.

The plantation's rice was lumpy low-grade stuff, and the price was higher than the price of good rice on the outside. At the first of each month, the plantation issued us rice tickets, which we could redeem one by one during the month. The only other kind of food available was salt fish of the worst quality, and they set the price on that as high as gold. If anyone so much as demurred, the overseers exercised their rods like the northern rain.

Thus, besides malaria, dysentery became chronic among the rubber workers. The less cautious took on the appearance of bags of skin and bones. Their bodies gradually grew more and more emaciated until they withered and died, and became fertilizer for the capitalists' rubber trees.

Then there were those who risked going up to the clinics in each village to ask for medicine. The French male nurses gave them IPK to drink, and they would return and vomit until their faces turned pale. Or the nurses would tell them to fast for several days to "arrest the development" of the dysentery germs. The women workers were forced to sleep with the medical personnel. Whether cured or still sick, the women workers were kept and imposed upon until the French nurses grew bored and sent them back to work.

We were supposed to have Sunday off, but on that day we had to do cleanup work around our housing area, including the barracks of the foremen and the private houses of the French overseers. It added up to five hours of unpaid work per person. So there was not one real day of rest in the whole year.

Our pay? Every *dong* was squeezed from us, too. In each village the overseers' families opened general merchandise shops with extremely high prices. If one did not buy essentials there, such as needles and thread, or envelopes, it was still not possible to go elsewhere to buy them. These shops usually doubled as gambling centers where people played coin games. The games were only open the first nights after each payday. Some of the men were so addicted that they would sell their month's rations to try to recoup their losses. There was no way they could recover, though. They only fell in deeper. One man sold all his clothes but a sarong. When night fell, he just wrapped it around his body to sleep and let the mosquitoes and ox-flies fight over him.

At that time in some of the factories in Sai-gon the capitalist owners were setting up what workers referred to as cages for shutting up the young. They were usually small, dark rooms, stuffy and unlighted. The owners forced workers to bring their children and shut them up there while they went to work in the factory. The children would be hungry and would fight with each other. They came out covered from head to toe with urine and feces.

At Phu-rieng, however, Michelin did not set up this kind of "children's cages" for a very simple reason. Because of the wretched sanitary, medical and living conditions, children might be born, but they could not be reared there. Throughout the three years I was at Phu-rieng, never once did I hear the babbling of a young voice.

We often sang this song about our strange situation:

"What a mistake to enter the rubber lands,

Like life imprisonment without a jail."

The French, too, were certainly aware that Phu-rieng was a hell on earth for us. No one who came could stand it. We would either flee or turn against our masters. So, right at the entrance to the plantation, there was a guard post manned by green sash[2] troops commanded by French officers. The soldiers patrolled day and night. Whenever they found a worker outside the boundaries of the plantation, they would arrest him on the spot and turn him over to the overseers.

Even that was not enough to set their minds at rest. The imperialists also schemed to sow and deepen divisions among the various nationalities. The forest region of Phu-rieng was populated only by compatriots of the mountain minorities. Because of restraints imposed by the feudalists and the imperialists, they were at a very backward, impoverished level. The men rolled themselves primitive G-strings; the women added a piece of cloth to cover their bodies. Every day they slung baskets on their backs and went out in the forest to search for fruits and firewood. On rainy days they would hoe up a few plots of land to grow rice on terraced fields.

In normal times they would take spears and crossbows into the forest to hunt wild dogs and foxes. When the rice was harvested, however, they would do an about-face and lie about drinking wine and singing and wasting time in their houses. And so they needed salt and cloth.

Taking advantage of the backwardness and those needs, the imperialists threatened and enticed the mountain minorities to follow them. One of the first things they did was to play on the people's superstitious minds by making fire. It was not particularly difficult. All they had to do was pour permanganate and glycerine on cotton, and fire burst out. The mountain people thought the imperialists had miraculous powers, so some feared and admired them. They enticed the people, saying: "Whoever catches a runaway worker and turns him in to 'monsieur' will get a reward of salt and money from 'monsieur.' If you turn the worker loose, 'monsieur' will set fire to your house and your fields. 'Monsieur' has miraculous powers, so no one can hide anything from 'monsieur.'

Some of the people feared the imperialists or were taken in by them and did what they were told. During 1927 many workers escaped the overseers and the green sash troops at the Phu-rieng plantation, but they could not escape those misguided mountain people.

But deceit is still deceit. Later, we were able to convince the mountain people. When they understood what was going on, they helped workers escape the hands of the enemy. We took a vow of brotherhood with them, eating food and drinking wine to seal our pledge to regard each other as flesh and blood relatives. Having picked up some knowledge of medicine at the Phu-rieng infirmary, I would treat these compatriots whenever I found any of them ill. Many people were cured, so they gained confidence in me and were very grateful. Gradually we became very close, and whenever they had something they would give it to us—sometimes a chicken, sometimes an egg.

When the mountain people heard our explanations, they gradually began to understand. We spoke of fighting the French, and some who did not yet understand responded immediately, "We can't fight 'monsieur.' 'Monsieur' has miraculous powers." I asked what miraculous powers. They said that all "monsieur" need do was say "burn" and fire would spring up at once. So I used the same materials the French had used to deceive them. When they saw that, they laughed and shouted, "Oh, you're as clever as 'monsieur.' If heaven will allow us, we can fight 'monsieur.'"

Phu-rieng spread farther with each passing day. The rows of rubber saplings encroached little by little on the ancient forests, invading even the corn and rice fields of the mountain people, driving them deeper and deeper into the forests. So they understood all the more what we were saying. They lamented to me: "We are from the same family and love each other. But 'monsieur' is not a brother from our family. 'Monsieur' is so cruel. 'Monsieur' is forever taking the land of the 'savages.' How, then, are the 'savages' to live?"

From that time on, not only did the mountain people help us with all their hearts, but they also agreed with us that we must fight the French. When the resistance broke out, this region became a very good base for anti-French guerrillas.[3] A great many mountain youth from the Phu-rieng area enlisted in the infantry and achieved great exploits. And to this very day Phu-rieng is a firm base for the liberation troops in South Viet Nam.

Seeing clearly that if we were able to mobilize the mountain people elsewhere as we had at Phu-rieng we would be on very firm ground, in January 1929 I went over to the Dau-tieng rubber company area to help our brothers there develop sympathy between the Kinh[4] workers and our mountain compatriots. After the situation settled down there, the two sides grew close as flesh and blood, as they had at Phu-rieng. They helped each other and agreed to fight the French together.

But that came later. During this earlier period, Phu-rieng lay in the midst of several circles of patrols, guarded most strictly. Things were so hard for the workers that some went out into the forest, taking with them a length of rope, and hanged themselves from the branch of a tree to escape their debts. Others found ways to flee, either individually or in groups of two or three or a dozen.

Once I was witness to a scene where seven men who had fled were captured by soldiers, bound, strung together in a line, and led back to the manager. The manager ordered the soldiers in, then forced the escapees down on the ground and let the soldiers tramp on their ribs with their nail-studded boots. Standing outside I could hear the sound of bones snapping. When they had finished trampling them with their boots, they beat them another round with canes, then shackled them in a darkened building. In that dark house they always kept a nine-person shackle. The brothers had to raise their legs to fit them through the holes in the shackle. When they were done, the soldiers went indifferently out to the work area to watch the laborers and forgot all about the incident which had just taken place. A week later, when they decided to punish another worker by shackling him, they opened the door of the dark house. There were the seven men, dead and stiff, their legs still raised up and passed through the holes of the shackles.

Phu-rieng continued to grow with every passing day. More and more newly recruited workers arrived. The number of workers' villages rose to nine. The plantation had an auto garage, and there was a generator and a water-purifying machine in each village reserved for the use of the manager and the French overseers. But each month there were nearly a hundred workers whose names were inscribed on the death register.

The rubber saplings were brought from the nursery and set out in perfectly straight, evenly spaced rows. The young green leaves of the rubber trees were indeed beautiful to behold. They were also hideous, because, when you counted it up, each row was fertilized by the corpse of at least one laborer.

Of all those who lived with me at Phu-rieng I know of only one person, comrade Nguyen Manh Hong,[5] who is still alive. Our brothers left their corpses by the thousands to fertilize the capitalists' rubber trees. In sorrow we often sang this couplet:

"Oh, it's easy to go to the rubber and hard to return,
Men leave their corpses, women depart as ghosts."

Thinking back on it now, I understand profoundly how the more they are threatened and oppressed, the more impoverished proletarians will strengthen their sympathy for each other. The more proletarians are exploited, the more they develop a spirit of struggle. When they endure such suffering, when they live in the shadow of such threats, always worried that although they live today, tomorrow they may be dead, then there is nothing at all that will frighten them. It takes only one man to sing out a line and a hundred, a thousand, will follow.

The capitalist masters might use every kind of devil disguised as a man, might use every possible method to persuade us, but it was impossible. We, the rubber workers of Phu-rieng, held fast to our common determination to oppose them.

THE FIRST BATTLES
(1927–1928)

It is now nearly four full decades since I first set foot on the soil
of Phu-rieng, yet I can recall my mood at that time as clearly as if
it were burned into my mind. On all four sides was the ancient,
untouched forest, empty of bird calls or the cold cries of the gib-
bons. Everywhere nothing but weeds, dust, and thorns. When we
jumped down from the truck there were only about a hundred
and fifty of us from Ha-nam left. When we left Hai-phong there
had been who knows how many of us. It had been those numbers
which lessened the sense of aloneness. But now, after we had been
divided by fives and by sevens, there were only this number of us
from the same part of the country brought together to Phu-rieng, a
place which held no promise of anything good whatsoever.

Did the surroundings at Phu-rieng weigh heavily on my heart?
No! Those forests and mountains, deserted though they were, were
still my country. Even today, this very minute, if the organization
directed me to return there, I would go at once, and would stay to
do whatever task my superiors gave me quite happily. The scenery
at Phu-rieng disoriented us, true, but it did not weigh heavily on
our hearts.

What gave us a start, and put us on the defensive, was the people
who came out to meet us. The chief overseers in their khaki suits
stared at us, probing, assessing our every gesture. Their eyes lacked
the least hint of affection. Their faces were harsh and cold like fe-
rocious beasts gazing hungrily at their prey.

As we were standing waiting to present our papers at the desk,
I can still remember how the eyes of the overseers glided over us

like the blade of a thin, keen-edged razor. And then there was their tone of voice, a surly, hostile tone. Besides that, their boots with nail-studded soles and their rattan rods, which they waved about like snakes raising their heads, signaled an extremely cruel manner of dealing with us.

All those things gave us the feeling we had stumbled into a corner of hell. We drew closer together and discreetly attempted to fathom the scene and the people of Phu-rieng. Suspicions in our hearts grew ever greater. Gradually we formed the conviction that, "now that we have stumbled into this place, it's a life-or-death situation between us and them." So now there was only one road for us. The two hundred or so of us, having reached this place, would have to close ranks to oppose them and protect each other until we could escape their wickedness. So I thought, and I was determined to risk my life in one round with the gang of executioners at Phu-rieng.

It was not long before I found myself in a determined struggle with them. In fact it was the very next morning. It was July 1927. The owners of the Michelin company were applying a policy of brutal whippings. The manager was a certain Triai, a captain in the Foreign Legion, a French soldier. I should also make it clear that the manager, the assistant manager, and all the overseers were recruited from among the mercenary troops.

This Triai was very big, very strong, and his face was as cold and fierce as that of a jail keeper. He never cursed, he only beat. I never saw him go anywhere without taking along a rattan cane as big around as his thumb. Although he was the manager, he was always out snooping around the work area. Whenever we workers saw that tall, gaunt shadow shouldering a rattan rod, the shadow of this French Corsican (we had heard somewhere that he was from the island of Corsica), then we had to get ready to defend ourselves. He had beaten quite a few people to death with one hand.

The chief overseers under Triai's authority followed his example, and were no less cruel. For example, there was Valentin. He was also a huge soldier, an adventurer. He beat very harshly, always punching and kicking the worker to the point of real danger. Another one was Monte, famous as the most cruel of all the overseers at Phu-rieng. He would beat from morning to night, until he had worn out whole sheaves of rods. And then there was the assistant manager, who was an old first lieutenant. He had no wife or children. He did not beat; he just raped. He neither spared the young nor had pity on the old. He was tall with long arms, and looked quite like a gibbon. When his passions rose, he would rape the women workers right out in the forest, right in the work area.

The overseers commonly beat workers who had just arrived in order to intimidate them. That very first day at Phu-rieng, the overseers blew their whistles to summon us to an empty field to check the roll before we went out to work. When we got there we saw the overseers standing in place, their canes ready. On all four sides of the field stood black-skinned soldiers holding guns with fixed bayonets. Triai was standing right in the middle. He shouted to us to line up.

One youth with an upset stomach did not get into a straight line soon enough and Triai sprang toward him, drew back his leg and kicked the youth, rupturing his spleen. The incapacitated youth lay writhing at his feet. Straight-faced as if nothing had happened, he gave a sign to his subordinates. Valentin and Monte then came over and struck out with their rods, at once striking us and counting out the number of workers in a loud voice.

When they reached me, I raised both arms to protect my head and spoke up quickly: "The contract forbids beatings. Why are you beating us?" I thought that the worker Triai had just kicked was surely dead, and that if nothing was said now, when they had just beaten one person to death, then tomorrow it would be someone else's turn and eventually perhaps my own. If we did not speak out, then they would just keep on beating us.

Triai was standing nearby, and when he heard me protest he seemed astonished. His whole pack of underlings also stared and stopped their beatings. The scene of riot and confusion stopped dead still for a moment. Triai approached me, glaring. I stared

back at him. Triai chuckled calmly, maliciously: "What contract?"
He drew the words out haughtily.

"The contract you signed with us; what else? The law forbids
you to beat us, yet here you are doing it anyhow. Look, you've
already killed one person!" I pointed to the youth who had been
kicked and was lying on the ground. With no sign of regret, Triai
turned his head, still chuckling: "And if we still beat you, what are
you planning to do to us?"

I was adamant: "If you keep up the beatings, we'll take you to
court. You're violating the law!"

Triai stared at me angrily. Suddenly he struck me hard on the
head with his rod and shouted: "Donnez la cadeuille! (Let him feel
the club.)" At once French and Vietnamese overseers alike began
caning me from left and right and kicking me with their hobnailed
boots. As the rain of blows fell, the scene grew twice as riotous as
before. I was beaten by Triai and Monte themselves. At the beginning I was still standing, encircling my head with my arms to
protect it. After they beat me to the ground, I drew myself up into
a ball, using my legs to protect my stomach and chest. The two of
them kept raining down blows.

Meanwhile the other workers broke and ran. The black-skinned
soldiers standing around the perimeter fired their guns into the
air. Most of the workers had to turn back, running in confusion
in the empty field, shielding themselves with their arms, dodging
the blows and kicks. A small number, a very few, risked their lives
by dashing past the encircling black-skinned soldiers and running
straight out into the forest. Some of the soldiers were sent to chase
them down. Their shouts were no different from those of hunters
chasing wild animals. Since the workers who fled did not know the
paths, they could not get away. The soldiers rounded them up and
dragged them back, beating them as they came.

By then I had passed out. I have no idea how much longer they
continued beating me. When I came to, I found myself in a dark
house with my legs held apart by shackles. I felt as if every spot on
my whole body had been hit. When I felt gently with my hands, I

discovered that I had wet, sticky blood all over me. Triai had used some of the black-skinned soldiers to throw me in here and shackle me. He had told them to guard me carefully and give me nothing to eat. The fact was that, even if they had thrown rice and their stinking, rotten salt fish in to me, I still couldn't have swallowed it. I would regain consciousness for a while, then pass out again. Even when I was conscious, I was in a daze.

That night, a worker they were using as a servant took pity on me, stole the key, some bread, and a bowl of milk, and brought the food to me. He waited until the black-skinned soldier nodded off to sleep, then secretly opened the door and brought the things in to me. It was a very dangerous thing for him to do. If the Frenchmen had found out about it, they would have given him a hard time indeed. The servant, too, would have been shackled and beaten and thrown in the dark house with no food. Had we not been in the same situation of poverty, how could he have cared so much for me that he would risk his life that way? That night, he waited until I had finished eating, then sneaked out and got away. The next night, he felt around behind the dark house, discovered an opening at the top of the wall, and pushed some food in. Afraid I would not know it was there, he poked a stick in and prodded me.

After three days, Triai opened the door of the dark house and came in. He spread his legs and stood looking at me. He spread his arms, his hands on his hips, his big rattan rod hanging down from his index finger on a loop of string, dangling behind him. He watched me for a while, then, laughing malevolently, asked: "Do you still want to be so headstrong?"

I kept my mouth shut and did not give even half a word in reply. Nodding, Triai looked at my wounds, still black with blood. He called in the black-skinned soldier guarding the dark house and ordered him to undo my shackles. At first I could not stand steadily, so the soldier had to hold me under the arms and take me to the clinic in the workers' village. Triai had the nurse dress my wounds and let me change into clinic dress, then turned to leave. Before he left, however, he threatened me once more: "If you get so headstrong again, we'll beat you to death and leave you out in the forest. Do you understand?" I turned purple with rage, but kept my mouth shut.

While I was being held in the dark house and taken up to the clinic, Triai had driven my fellow workers out to the work area. After that first round of beatings to intimidate them, Triai urged the overseers to beat the workers unceasingly. He probably thought that he would take advantage of his position to keep on doing it. Monte and Valentin and their crew gave even fiercer beatings. Those who were beaten in that first round resigned themselves to retreating, trying to bear it, and waiting to see how things would work out.

We lost the first round, but we did not yield. I contained my shame and went out to work, but my heart was filled with anger and resentment. Every evening when we had returned from the work area and finished dinner, and whenever we had a free minute, we met for whispered discussions about how we could strike a blow in this "game" with the French. We were determined not to let them go on beating us forever. But discussions are only discussions, and we still had found no way to "play the game" with them.

At that time, all the rubber plantations were experiencing incidents between the workers and their French masters. The colonialists could hardly stop up their ears and forever pretend not to know anything. They had to issue a proclamation organizing an Inspectorate of Labor for all of Indochina, signed 19 July 1927.

The Inspectorate selected Delamarre, a French official, to come to Phu-rieng for an inspection. He was obviously an experienced Indochina hand and was quite fluent in Vietnamese.

When he came to inspect the clinic and met me while I was doing corvée labor nearby, Delamarre told me to show him around. At the time there were some thirty people in the clinic, about half of whom had been injured in beatings. Tran Van Chuyen's back was still covered with deep scars where a split cane had sliced into his flesh. Another brother from Village 3, named Vu Viet Thu, was in worse condition. Monte had given him fifty strokes with a stingray cane the day before. This variety of cane was ragged, and wherever it struck it ripped through skin and flesh. Delamarre told me to pull up Thu's shirt so he could see the wounds, still oozing yellow pus and giving off a nauseating fishlike odor.

After that, Delamarre continued his inspection. He told the workers they could denounce anything to him because the old administrator of Plantation Alpha did not know Vietnamese. They were still cautious when they directed Delamarre's attention to various places for investigation, however.

I secretly pointed out the dark house to him. Delamarre insisted on going in. It was nothing but a prison. The day before, Triai's crew had shackled Vu Viet Thu in there. That morning, when he got the news an inspector was coming, Triai finally released brother Thu to go to the clinic. In the cell sat the nine-person shackle and irons. It was an acute embarrassment for Plantation Alpha, and they did not know what to say. I signaled Delamarre to notice the building next door. Delamarre demanded to look inside, and Alpha overseers had to open the door. People were still imprisoned there. Just then Triai returned from the work area and followed the inspector in. Delamarre pointed out a man in shackles to Triai, who had the door opened wider so he could see. It was a worker from Village 2 who already had been shut up there for a week. He was stark naked except for a G-string. After being shut up for so long, he was pale as a sheet, his body was gaunt and filthy, and his legs were raised up in the air to fit through the shackles. Old Delamarre had them help the shackled man stand up. Searching over his body, Delamarre found six scars from a stingray cane on the man's back. He had a nurse called in. This man, Phong, from Tan-uyen in Bien-hoa Province, was nicknamed the "cruel nurse." His flattery was so cynical that the old Alpha administrator grew embarrassed and tried to cover it over by saying, "This is no clinic. Take him somewhere else." So the nurse opened the shackles and freed the man.

Delamarre's inspection continued for a full day. He searched every nook and cranny. He even went out to the most distant work area, writing down everything he saw. Indeed there was no lack of documentation. There were thousands of violations of the law that he had to write down. The farthest corner was full of them.

That night the plantation owners gave Delamarre a banquet, and the next morning he went back to Sai-gon. We waited and waited to see whether anything would change, but absolutely nothing out of the ordinary happened. I even grew worried that Delamarre might have told Triai and his crew that I had pointed out places for him to inspect. Yet I did not see any difference in Triai's attitude toward me.

It was only a great while later that I finally understood what that character Delamarre had been up to. The occupation of labor inspector was for fortune seekers. There was no place you could go in those days and not find thousands of violations of the law. Inspectors would write down as many violations as they could in their notebooks, then go bargain with the owners. The owners had nothing to fear from the labor inspectors. The government was their government, and everything was fine so long as they could keep matters quiet. So, if there had to be an inspection, then there would be an inspection. Afterwards, they would still invite the inspectors to a banquet. And when it came time for the inspectors to leave, the owners would line their hands with suitable amounts of money and gifts. Nothing was disturbed.

As for those who had informed him of places he should look, such as me, Delamarre kept that secret to himself. He wanted to prolong his profitable working days in Indochina. He also wanted the laborers in other places to give him the documentation he needed to bargain with the owners. If he had denounced me, the news would have been passed on to other places, and the people there would have been on guard, making it hard for him to learn anything about the situation, or leaving him knowing very little. In that case, bargaining with the owners would have been quite difficult. That was the inspection game those French scoundrels played!

In early October of that year—in other words, three months later—another group of new workers came down from the North. The French owners set up Village 2 with 120 workers. As before,

Triai had them beaten the very first morning they went out to work in order to intimidate them. That day the overseer who beat them most brutally was none other than Monte. The brothers were furious, but they could find no way to retaliate.

One of the new arrivals was Nguyen Dinh Tu. When he was up north, Tu had a reputation as an adventurer. He told everyone, "They are men; we are men, too. How can we let them keep on beating us forever! Set a careful ambush, knock off one of them right away, and it will scare the wits out of the rest of them. 'Kill one man, ten thousand men fear you.'" He came over to Village 1 and asked for me. At that time I, too, thought that was the right thing to do. Tu went right back to Village 2 and told everyone to contribute some money for a dedication banquet. Everyone did as he said.

On payday each person contributed one *dong* to buy beef, wine, incense, and candles. When it grew dark, some of the workers from Village 2 followed Tu out into the forest. They put up an altar and set out wine and food for a dedication meal. Each person took a knife, drew blood from his finger, let it fall into the bowl of wine, then took a pledge to live or die together. When they finished the pledge, they took up the tray of wine and drained the bowls until they were quite drunk.

About this time the owners grew suspicious of me and made me come work as custodian at the clinic. I took immediate advantage of this opportunity to pick up whatever knowledge of medicine I could and to find every possible chance to supply medicines to the workers.

One morning I was passing out quinine to the workers to guard against malaria when Monte came. The roll call began. As usual, Monte struck everyone on the head with his cane, counting out loud in French. The workers pretended to take no special notice of it and just raised their hands to protect their heads. As Monte went deeper into the ranks, he came near Tu, who suddenly shouted, "Brothers! Kill him!" The freshly sharpened crescent-shaped axe in Tu's hand flashed up, then slashed down. Monte ducked just in time. The axe sliced into the flesh of the overseer's shoulder. He spun around and fled to his bungalow, so scared of the smell of blood that he ran powerfully in spite of the wound. Tu brandished his axe and gave chase, shouting, "After him! After him!" A number of the others raised their picks and pruning knives and chased off the panic-stricken foremen. Monte could not get back to his quarters to get his gun. He had just reached the wooden stairs outside his bungalow when the blades of nine axes descended on him. The final blow split off half his face.[1]

The French foremen and the black-skinned soldiers were terrified and came rushing out in great disorder, firing their guns wildly. All the workers ran off into the forest. When the soldiers came to search the forest, the workers fled further away.

When Triai arrived, he called out more soldiers, surrounded the workers on all four sides and chased them down. He caught forty or fifty people and brought them back. Those who came in range of his own gun he shot dead. The bodies of the dead were buried right out in the forest, and even those still writhing in pain were buried alive. Later their bodies would fertilize the latex-bearing rubber trees for the capitalists.

There were also a number of workers who managed to evade encirclement by the black-skinned soldiers but in the end could not escape, either. The savage mountain soldiers cut off their heads, sliced off their ears, and brought them back to the plantation for a bounty. Others were shot and wounded, brought back by gun-toting black-skinned soldiers and left outside on the veranda of the clinic. However Triai would not let the nurse bandage their wounds. They lost so much blood that they also died.

Those who were picked up in the forest were taken to Bien-hoa and turned over to the Secret Police. They were savagely tortured in an attempt to learn who the instigator was. Finally they found out it was brother Tu. The Bien-hoa court sentenced him to death and handed down life sentences to two other workers involved in the plot with Tu. These brothers were very proud. They admitted what they had done, and did not try to blame anyone else.

After Monte was killed, Triai, wanting to take revenge for his lackey, had the workers repressed savagely. Valentin, wanting to avenge his friend, beat us all the more. He also directed the Vietnamese foremen to beat us as he did. If any of them failed to follow his instructions, he would beat them, too. Counting only the victims of this one man, the number beaten to death in this quest for vengeance rose into the dozens. Whoever died, Valentin had their corpse buried right in the grove of rubber seedlings.

Triai suspected me, too. He had me called up and asked threatening questions to see if I was involved in the affair in any way. I answered, "I don't know." My living quarters were as much as three kilometers from Village 2. The workers there had just arrived from the North and did not know me. Triai grabbed my hand and looked at the end of the index finger, but he could not find any sign of my having cut my finger at the dedication banquet. With no concrete evidence, he had to release me.

After two attempts to argue back and fight back were both repressed fiercely, people's spirits fell, especially the second time, when quite a number of people were killed. It had reached the point where people did not dare look straight ahead as they walked. But the spirit of affection amidst the mutual pain did not fall; it increased. Workers often came to visit those who were seriously ill and those who had been crippled. Occasionally, when someone was going to Bien-hoa, they would contribute some money to give to those who had been imprisoned.

At the end of the year there was another incident. One of the Vietnamese foremen in Village 2 was Nguyen Van Chanh. Although he was a foreman, he was a good man who did not brutalize the workers. Every time he came out to the work area to keep watch, he would stand guard so we could slow down the pace of our work. The French noticed and were constantly spying, but they never caught us red-handed. During this period, their policy was to keep the pressure on us by beating us, and they made every effort to encourage the Vietnamese foremen to do as they did.

One morning Valentin came out to the work area and meticulously inspected each hole for the new trees to see if it was dug with straight sides. Was the dirt all cleaned out? He made the workers raise their hoes so he could see if they were keeping them sharp. He was just looking for trouble.

Naturally he called Chanh to him and raged, "Is this the way you watch the workers! Look how sloppily these holes are dug, and the hoes are all dull. Come here. Look at them." He pulled the blade of a hoe from the hand of a worker standing nearby and shoved it right in Chanh's face. The blade was only nicked the slightest bit. "You can go search the whole plantation and you won't find a hoe that's in better shape," Chanh retorted. "If people keep it in this condition, that's doing very well!"

Valentin continued to curse him angrily. And Chanh grew furious as he was cursed. Then Valentin drew back his foot and drove it straight into Chanh's vital organs. Kicked so suddenly he could not avoid the blow, he fell straight to the ground. He passed out at once, his face a dark purple, his eyes rolling backward, saliva drooling from his mouth. The workers stopped their work and gathered around. Valentin, crude as ever, yelled, "So! Want to pretend you're hurt, do you? I'll give you a few kicks so you'll know what the real thing is like." He kicked Chanh several more times. The workers were infuriated and said, "The man's passed out and slobbering and you still beat him! Look at him. Can you tell if he's dead or alive?"

"He's dead! Impertinent idiot!" Valentin let fly with one more curse, then swung his club on his shoulder and left.

The workers gathered around and carried Chanh to the clinic. But the blow had struck a critical spot, rupturing his spleen. Chanh lay moaning for a while, then died. He left behind a wife and two small children.

That night I went around to mobilize all the barracks. I thought that if we let them keep on beating us, they would gradually kill us all off. Yet it would not accomplish anything to act in the risky way we had the two earlier times. This time we would take the matter to court and see what happened. When I went around to talk to the workers, everyone agreed. I went to see Chanh's wife. She also agreed to sign the complaint. So I wrote out the complaint and showed Mrs. Chanh where to make her mark. Early the next morning we sent the complaint to the Bien-hoa court.

The law of the French is strange indeed. They have all manner of examinations, autopsies, and questioning of witnesses. They drag things on for weeks. When they are done with that stage, they have the questioning of the plaintiff and the defendant, which goes on for months. Then there is another very long period which they say is for preparation of the indictment. Only after that do they try the case. This surely gave the plantation owners plenty of time to arrange the necessary bribes on Valentin's behalf.

When the case finally did come to trial in Bien-hoa, we had prepared the witnesses carefully. Every sentence of testimony was in agreement; Valentin had indeed kicked a man to death. When it came his turn to speak, Valentin also admitted that he had kicked him. His testimony went like this: "This Chanh did not regard the work site as his responsibility. When I spoke to him, he wouldn't listen, but argued back. I kicked him once to bring him into line. I had meant to kick him in the buttocks, but unfortunately he dodged and the blow struck him in his vital organs. I didn't mean to kick him there." After that, the Michelin company's French lawyer argued very spiritedly for Valentin.

The trial took five months for the investigation and three days to reach a verdict. The grass on brother Chanh's grave at Phu-rieng was drenched with the waters of the rainy season and had grown lush and green. In the end the Bien-hoa court concluded that, with a misdirected foot, Valentin had kicked a man to death. It was negligent manslaughter. He was sentenced to pay five *piaster* damages to the widow of the ill-fated man.

Five *piaster* for the life of a man! The price was cheap, yet also extremely high. What of the dozens of others who had died before Chanh? No one received so much as a *xu* for them!

When one thought about it, though, considering that the whole matter had been brought out in public, before a court of law, and that was the only punishment, the whole thing seemed most cynical and unjust. Experience had now taught us that we would have to take care of our own affairs, and not place any confidence in the courts of the imperialists. And so we met one more defeat.

Before we realized it, we had been at Phu-rieng for over half a year. Around Village 1, Village 2, and Village 3 vast areas of the jungle had been cleared out. The bright red earth gleamed vermillion in the sun. Here and there rubber saplings transplanted from the nursery had put out deep green shoots. How many of us had departed this life to create that scene! Our compatriots had died like sand, like dust, and their flesh and bones had decayed and become a part of that vermillion earth.

After the passage of a half year, we also had more experience in methods of struggle with the capitalist masters. I do not know who started it, but a new form of struggle appeared: We would pass the word to slow the tempo of our work. At the time the workers did not really recognize this as a form of struggle, nor did they call it a slowdown. They simply said, "Why should we knock ourselves out working for them?"

One person was assigned to look out for the French foreman and the Vietnamese foreman who tagged along with him. Whenever they were looking the other way, we worked indifferently. Hoes rose and fell, but no one bothered to scoop up the dirt. They just left it wherever it fell. Knives chopped on wood for hours without felling a single tree. The overall productivity of the plantation fell perceptibly. The overseers grew increasingly upset, yet there was no way they could keep a close enough watch on things. Whenever they happened to be at a particular place, we worked fine there. But as soon as they left, the workers passed the word to slow down again.

As we gradually gained experience, we began to tell each other how to kill rubber saplings. These saplings were brought from the nursery and planted in small, skillfully woven bamboo baskets. We would dig the soil out of the basket, use a small knife to cut nearly half way through the main root, then plant it carefully in the hole. The root would become waterlogged. A week later the root would rot. Gradually the tree would lose its leaves, and even if it lived it would be weak and would have to be dug up and replaced with another tree. The French did not become suspicious, as we only slit the root of about one tree in three.

During this period a number of the workers who could not bear the living situation continued to flee. They might depart in ones and twos, or they might talk it over and get half a dozen people to leave at once. Before going, each person set aside a bit of food and a canister of matches. They waited until they had received their pay, then fled. On the long path through the fierce forest, they had their hatchets and sharp sap-drawing knives for protection. There were few weeks when there were not two or three incidents like this.

Some groups got away and some did not. The savage mountain militia caught fleeing rubber workers when they could, cut off their heads, and brought them back to the plantation to turn in for a bounty. Nevertheless only a few months afterward we were able to eat a meal of brotherhood with the people of the surrounding villages and make friends with them. Afterwards, we convinced the militia to let any fleeing workers they might meet pass on.

The slowdowns and escapes forced the French owners to change their attitudes about how to deal with us. It was at this point, in 1928, that Vasser, a renegade missionary priest, came to take Triai's place. Vasser had joined the army and become a first lieutenant after leaving the monastery. He was short and fat. He wore glasses and was as lazy as a sleeping cat. As soon as Vasser arrived, he issued a declaration prohibiting overseers from beating workers. Of course, when out of Vasser's sight the overseers kept right on with their beatings. Vasser's prohibition was nothing but empty words.

As for the workers' living conditions, Vasser allowed distribution of rice which was not stale. And the salt fish was not so often rotten. He allocated funds to buy clothes and hats so the workers could form a *cheo* group.[2] He bought a lion's head for the dance and even bought instruments and drums so we could form traditional music ensembles. And, for anyone who did not like *cheo* or music, he had a soccer team.

In the area of working conditions, Vasser announced a piecework system. He said, "Whoever finishes early may come back early."

Looking only at his style, one would think he was quite good. In fact, he was extremely cunning. He knew there was no way he could keep close enough watch to prevent slowdowns. He knew, too, that there was no way to prevent workers from fleeing. Besides, some progressive newspapers of the period, such as *Than Chung [Common Spirit]*,[3] published a number of articles mentioning scenes of ill-treatment at Phu-rieng, and hence forcing the colonialists to act more shrewdly. Then, too, they had to think of their balance sheets. If they kept on in the old way, they would lose thousands.

Vasser thought that setting quotas was the cleverest method. But the quotas he set were very high. Those who dug holes to plant the trees had to dig forty-five holes, even though an average digger could only complete forty holes a day. Those who planted saplings had to plant fifteen, whereas an average person could only plant twelve a day. Almost all the quotas Vasser set for various other kinds of work were similarly high.

In early 1928 there was one other event worth recounting. That was an inspection tour by Bui Bang Doan, representative of the Hue court to the colonial authorities in the South. According to laws of the French and the court of Khai Dinh[4] at the time, northerners working in the South were regarded as working on French soil, because the South was a direct colony. The emperor continued to regard northerners working here as his "children," however, so he had an obligation to look after them. The newspapers had said so much that he could not stop his ears to the situation. Bui Bang Doan was thus appointed to come down to inspect.

Bui Bang Doan was an honorable man, and wanted to find out the truth. The servants and cooks in the manager's bungalow let us know about his visit several days ahead of time. We had a discussion and selected a person to tell him how bad the situation was. For my own part, after our experience at the Bien-hoa trial, I did not place much hope in this tour.

As we had expected, one day we saw a poster with instructions that we were to be let off early so we could clean up our quarters. For hours on end the overseers pressed the workers to clean things up and set up beds. Wherever a building had a leaky roof, they passed out new steel sheets and made us repair it. The walls were painted with fresh whitewash. The entire place was very clean to the eye. The next morning the overseers did not blow their whistles to assemble us for roll call until just before time to go to work. Even the cruelest of the French foremen, like the Le Bonne brothers, were empty-handed, their canes and clubs put away somewhere. We told each other that the inspector must be about to come.

Just as we had supposed, about nine o'clock the manager, Vasser, drove up in a car, bringing Bui Bang Doan to the plantation. Bui Bang Doan went to the trouble of inspecting even the clinic and the tree nursery. He went all the way out to the work area to see the workers on the job. Everywhere he saw what appeared to be a pleasant life. Vasser's crew were quite shrewd. They had prepared some of their lackeys to dog Bui Bang Doan's heels. Whatever he asked, they answered, as if they were workers.

But at Village 3 the workers had chosen brother Ty to denounce plantation living conditions on their behalf. Vasser stood listening silently to Ty as if he didn't understand anything. Ty told about the docking of our pay as punishment and about the daily beating of workers. Vasser spread his hands in surprise. He explained to everyone standing around, "What did I know of that? I ordered an end to the beatings." He asked the person standing beside him, "Isn't that right? I forbade them from the first day I came, didn't I?" He laughed as he spoke, but in his eyes there was a gleam of contempt and derision. Brother Ty detailed the number of hours a worker had to put in each day: including the time to go out to the work area and return to the barracks, everyone had to work from eleven to thirteen hours. "If so, that's much too hard," Vasser interjected. Several other workers picked up where Ty left off and denounced the health care, the short rations, and the accidents which were always occurring on the job. Vasser stood listening, nodding, sometimes adding a comment: "I'll have to look into that," or, "That's the first I've heard about that."

Finally Vasser gave a short little laugh and took Bui Bang Doan out to the car. As soon as he had gone, life at Phu-rieng returned to normal, or even grew worse. The French overseers beat us more savagely than before, and cursed, "You mothers! You think you're so smart with your denunciations. We'll teach you when to keep your mouths shut." Those French overseers who did not curse the workers cursed the Hue court: "Those mothers! They can't fuck with me. I'll just beat you and see what they can do about it."

So, just as a number of us had suspected, the denunciations of the living conditions at Phu-rieng turned out to be a shameful defeat. The members of the Hue imperial court were only valets for the French. However honorable Bui Bang Doan might be, there was nothing he could do to the French.[5]

Not only did we gain nothing from the inspection, but indeed the results were fatal. A week later brother Ty suddenly turned up missing. After several days, noticing all the birds in the forest twittering around one tree, we went out together and found Ty dead, hanging by the neck from the limb of a tree, his corpse swollen, liquid running from it. We knew that Ty had not committed suicide, but had been lynched by lackeys of the capitalists. We resigned ourselves to swallow our anger, however, and wait for another opportunity.

Our attempts to oppose the plantation masters had not worked out at all. They did not yield to argument. When we killed one cruel overseer, they sent in others no less cruel. When we took them to court, we were defeated. And when we denounced them to French or Vietnamese labor inspectors, once again we were defeated.

In assessing our struggles from late 1927 to early 1928, we found that they had brought no results to speak of, with the exception of the slowdowns and the secret sabotage, which had forced the enemy to change their attitudes a bit.

All the same, through those various struggles our mutual understanding increased, our affection for each other grew more firm, and we gained confidence in and esteem for each other. All these factors united the workers at Phu-rieng into a bloc, ready for a new wave of victorious struggle, if only that new wave had clear-sighted leadership. To put it another way, the movement at Phu-rieng lacked only a head.

By April 1928 that head for the workers of Phu-rieng had begun to take shape. Our struggles, and those of the workers at such other plantations as Sa-cam and Sa-cat, echoed throughout the South.

THE PARTY COMES
TO PHU-RIENG

Our struggles drew the attention of Ngo Gia Tu,[1] one of the first
Communists in Viet Nam. Brother Tu had come south to work in
1927. In 1928 he delegated Nguyen Xuan Cu, alias Vinh, one of his
comrades, to go up to Phu-rieng to work in the rubber workers
movement and to build up an infrastructure for the Revolutionary Youth League. Cu was from the North, a student at the Buoi
school (now the Chu Van An school).[2] Though he had student
roots, brother Cu understood that if he wanted to make revolution
he would have to go among the worker and peasant masses and
learn from them to be able to fulfill his responsibility. He came to
Phu-rieng and asked to work as houseboy for the overseer Lebonne, chief of Village 3.

At the time the French hated and suspected me and transferred me
to the clinic to clean up and do the laundry. They wanted to cut me
off from the old Ha-nam workers who really believed in me. So, from
then on, I had to live at the clinic. The work was hard and complex,
but I learned what I could from it. After only a few months working
at the clinic I knew how to give intramuscular and intravenous injections. I also knew how to use the common drugs. The head nurse,
whose name was Phong, was short with very dark skin. He would
laugh maliciously while he stared evenly at you. Phong beat the patients resoundingly, and whenever any women workers were ill and
came to the clinic, he always raped them. Many times I stopped him,
he beat me, and I hit back. I had long been famous at the plantation
for my obstinacy, and I was not about to submit to him.

Brother Cu heard of my attitude and of all the struggles I had been involved in before, so he held me in high esteem. He sought me out to make friends. He invited me back to his room and we exchanged confidences. He was very poised, and every time he explained something to me he went slowly, explaining each detail so I had a thorough understanding of all he had said.

Cu also worked cautiously. Before he propagandized anyone, he researched and investigated the person carefully. Within a short time the number of people he had propagandized and brought into the Revolutionary Youth League had risen to four, including me and three other comrades: Ta, Hong and Hoa. Cu's style of work had a great influence on me after that.

The things that Cu explained to us were very practical. They were in direct response to the impasse we faced at the time. They helped us discover the reasons for the failure of our previous efforts, and at the same time gave each person confidence in the new methods of struggle. For the first time I understood how revolutionary theory was related to the revolutionary movement. The teachings of the old masters of Marxism penetrated my heart still more deeply: "Without revolutionary theory there is no revolutionary movement," and "When theory thrusts deep into reality it becomes a material strength." Nevertheless I really only understood the principles which lay behind these slogans a long time later, after I had passed through the "university" of the revolution, in prison. At the time I simply knew that, thanks to Cu's explanations, I was like a person groping his way along a rugged road who suddenly sees a sheaf of blazing torches brilliantly lighting the way.

Cu passed on to us a great many experiences and concrete methods of struggle. He helped us to understand what an organized struggle is, how to select the crucial slogans, how to set up a leadership committee, how to organize our defenses, how much food to set aside, and so forth. We were hearing most of this for the very first time.

Comrade Cu had our complete affection and confidence. He had not been with us for long, yet the rubber workers were drawn to him as iron to a magnet. I still remember how we would gather after we had eaten in the evenings to hear Cu speak. On cool evenings when the moon was bright, we would go out in the yard together and sit on the ground. At that hour the manager, assistant manager, and overseers had their heads buried in their fancy, proper houses, having a good time with their wives and children. So no one discovered our activities. We sat and listened, entranced. After talking about struggle experiences, Cu would tell us about the Soviet Union, about the land where workers like us had taken complete control, about the struggles of workers around the world.

Often the hour grew quite late, but there was not one of us who wanted to be the first to leave. Anyone who had the misfortune to be sick and could not come to hear Cu speak was very sorry. Gradually our zest for life grew. A sense of confidence in the coming struggle, and in our lives afterward, rose in our hearts.

While he was propagandizing the workers at Phu-rieng, Cu maintained close contact with Ngo Gia Tu, who was then in Cho-lon. The person who took up the task of liaison at that time was Ty, a woman worker who came from the village of Chi-lai, An-lao District, Kien-an Province. Sister Ty was tiny and elegant. She had large round eyes which glowed an expressive black, mirroring the determination and courage in her heart. She kept up her work until the big 1930 struggle.

On a couple of occasions Cu had me go to Cho-lon. Cu had a special affection for me. In part it was because I was direct and loyal by nature, and in part it was because I was the first person he had recruited. Besides this sense of spontaneous comradeship, we shared the vows of brotherhood we had taken. After our exchanges of thoughts about the tyranny the capitalist owners were imposing on the plantation, our hostility toward them increased. We asked two men who worked in the machine shop to forge two hatchet blades with the word "justice" engraved on the face of each. Cu and I exchanged these two finely honed hatchets. It revealed my immaturity, yet at the same time it expressed our intent.

Before we realized it, Cu had been at Phu-rieng for the better part of a year. The number of people grouped around us grew daily. At the time the labor movement in our country was seething. In those circumstances the working class had an urgent need for their own party, a tightly organized party with a system of leadership from top to bottom, a party with the correct theoretical direction to be able to lead the movement to victory.

Thus, on the basis of the Revolutionary Youth League and the New Viet Nam Revolutionary Party, three Communist groups—the Indochinese Communist party, the Communist party of Annam, and the Indochinese Communist League—were formed within the space of a few months. These were the revolutionary organizations of our working class which were later, on 3 February 1930, unified by Nguyen Ai Quoc into the Vietnamese Communist party (later changed to the Indochinese Communist party), the vanguard party of the working class and of our nation.

During this period, before the unification of the Indochinese Communist party, all the communist groups were engaged in positive activities, building bases among the masses, organizing new branches, pushing forward the movement among workers and laboring people in every quarter, building an unprecedentedly powerful revolutionary movement.

Ngo Gia Tu was one of the people in the Revolutionary Youth League who actively pushed those first efforts to build a party of the working class. Brother Tu gave Nguyen Xuan Cu the task of founding a branch of the Indochinese Communist party at Phu-rieng. Cu gave the rules and regulations of the party to a number of workers at Phu-rieng to study. I was one of them.

The Phu-rieng branch was officially founded one night in October 1929. In all, six of us went together into the forest behind Village 3 for the founding ceremony. We lit some candles and hung a hammer and sickle flag on a large tree, wrapping it around the trunk. It was a clear, bright moonlit night and the weather was quite chilly, yet I felt hot all over. You could tell from his face how moved Cu was as he announced, on behalf of his superiors, the reason for the meeting. Our right hands clenched tightly, we raised them above our heads in a salute to the flag.

After the salute, Cu read the oath. It was so long ago that I cannot remember exactly what the words were, but I still remember quite clearly the spirit of the oath. It included the following points:

- To be loyal to our class and to the party until death.

- To preserve party secrets to the end. If we were captured by the enemy we were not to confess, even if it meant we were tortured to death.

- To integrate ourselves into the masses, and to stand shoulder to shoulder in struggle.

- To set aside every other faith and believe only in communism.

- To combine our strength in the struggle, first for the national liberation revolution and afterwards for the socialist revolution, advancing towards a world of great harmony.

We all raised our hands in the air and took the vow. After the oath, we all shook hands and called each other "comrade." It is hard to describe how I felt at that moment. At that hour I had officially come into the family of Communists, of revolutionaries. There was something about being called "comrade" for the first time that gave me an extraordinary feeling of warmth and affection. I felt as if my strength had doubled. From then on, the minds and hands of these comrades would help me and lead me forward. My heart felt light, floating, as if I were being lifted up. My ears grew hot, and my eyes were so misty I could not see my comrades clearly.

So it was that the Phu-rieng branch was founded. The four comrades besides me and Cu were Ta, Hong, Hoa, and Doanh. Cu was the secretary. I was assigned the task of organizing youth for a Red Guards unit. Ta was responsible for Village 2. He was a tall man from Ha-noi, very poised, and the workers had great confidence in him. At that time Hong was a driver at the car garage, so he was given responsibility for the labor union. Hong was quite courageous, but he was quiet and gentle like a girl. When he exchanged confidences with us, he often expressed the wish that the village of Thi-cau in Bac-ninh, his home village, could have a party branch, too. Doanh was the leader of Village 3. In contrast to Hong, Doanh was tall and walked with great self-assurance. He was bold, a hearty eater, and a loud talker. Hoa also worked at the car garage and helped Hong in the task of mobilizing the drivers and machine shop workers there. Afterwards, whenever the branch met we usually used an empty room in the overseer's house where Cu worked or the pharmacy at the clinic where I worked.

The work at that time was still rather helter-skelter, but it was very practical. The branch paid attention to the workers' food and living quarters and to each person's family life in order to work out problems quickly and settle them peacefully.

Because sister Ty carried out her communications work so well, Ngo Gia Tu was in regular contact with us. He secretly sent books and newspapers for us to read. The newspapers were *Thanh nien giai phong* [*Liberation Youth*] and *Humanité*, the official publication of the French Communist party. *Humanité* was written in French, and since I had some knowledge of that language I was responsible for translating the main articles for the others to read—articles on the world situation, the situation in France, and experiences and lessons from struggle. We learned a great deal from *Humanité*. The French Communists were our brothers, comrades with a common enemy: the capitalists, the colonialists, the imperialists who were ruling us. Their newspaper reached us at just the right time and was precious spiritual food for us, since we party members at Phu-rieng had a low level of theoretical understanding and lacked experience in struggle.

The party's line and course of action at that time were for the most part laid out for us by Cu. Among the major components of the party course of action which Cu explained, there was only one which bothered me. Cu had spoken about the problem of fields and farmers in our country. He had emphasized the necessity of confiscating all the land held by religious organizations. I felt it was correct to take back factories and mines for the workers and to take back land from the landlords for the farmers. But why should we also take religious land holdings to divide among the people? Those lands belonged to God. What did the crops and interest used to pay for religious services have to do with the revolution? Indeed, it was the lessons inculcated in me during those years in church schools which made me wonder about this.

I asked Cu about it. Right away he asked me how I had lived when I was at the Hoang Nguyen seminary. I answered that it had been a very hard life. Then he asked me what kind of life the tenant farmers around the mission seemed to have. I responded that their lives seemed even harsher than mine. Cu laughed quietly, then explained to me who a landlord was and who a farmer was. He said that the nature of rent paid to the mission was no different from the nature of rent paid to a landlord. He emphasized that it was necessary to reclaim that religious land and divide it among the farmers, though naturally a certain amount of land would be left for pagodas and churches to use for their services. But it would be absolutely forbidden to use this land to exploit the poor. Cu's clear, simple, concrete explanation dissolved my doubts. From then on I believed him with all my heart and mind, without the slightest ambiguity.

Since we had just been enlightened, those of us in the branch were extremely enthusiastic. Secret party organizations—the trade union and the Red Guards unit—were set up. The party branch competed with the owners for control of mass organizations. Many legal organizations—the mutual aid and assistance association, sports and art groups—were set up under branch control. Work went on at a fast pace.

In general every struggle was under party direction. Yet there were many ultra-left activities, too, and I myself was involved in some of them. At that time there was a French nurse named Vaillant at the clinic. He had originally been a sailor and knew nothing at all about medicine. He did not even know how to give an injection. He was a highly paid idiot. On the job all he did was sit and wave his hand to tell us what to do. If something displeased him in the least, he would launch into loud curses and denunciations. Once he called me "savage." I was furious at him. Vaillant sprang threateningly toward me. That is how the fight broke out. I put up my hand to ward off his slap, then took advantage of the situation to land a blow on Vaillant's jaw. He fell, smashing one of the clinic beds. Then he sprang up and ran into the office to get a gun. I fled. Vaillant fired several shots into the air but did not dare chase me. It was evening before I returned.

By that time the movement at Phu-rieng had gained strength. The imperialists were looking for some way to calm the movement, so Vaillant did not dare behave too fiercely. He just docked my pay four *dong* and pretended to patch up relations by saying, "The higher-ups like you, so they have decided not to throw you in prison!" I gave an evasive answer and thought to myself, "Your mother! Just try something and see what happens." There were a lot of incidents like that during this period.

Cu was exhausted from his efforts to shape the struggle in the proper way. From time to time Cu went back to Sai-gon to report to Ngo Gia Tu on the situation. Once Cu took me along with him. I got to meet Tu at his quarters on Lagrandière Street.

At that time, toward the end of 1929, the Indochinese Communist party was continuing to push the task of proletarianizing its cadres and party members. Tu was working as a coolie in Cho-lon, both to make a living and to establish a base for his activities. He lived in a tiny, cramped room with only a broken-down bed and a few changes of worn clothes. Yet within a few minutes after I met him, I could see that he was an extraordinarily warm-hearted person. On the outside there was nothing noteworthy about him. If anything, he was rather ugly, squat, and heavy-set with a round face and small eyes. But his manner of speaking was very unaffected and intimate. Tu's attitude toward younger comrades like me was open and friendly, leading everyone to love and trust him at once.

His way of speaking was very practical, not the least bit literary. "If we want to liberate ourselves," he told me, "we must liberate our class first. We are all members of that social class."

"To struggle for class liberation," he advised me, "we must integrate ourselves with the proletarian masses; we must be proletarianized."

Ngo Gia Tu's words moved me greatly. The more we talked, the fonder I became of him. I learned a great many useful things from this visit with him. He had a concrete understanding of the workers' struggle. He very carefully read the newspaper which we published secretly at Phu-rieng and especially liked the column on workers' activities. In that column we satirized certain bad habits and customs like gambling, drunkenness, and wife snatching. "This is good!" Tu said. "Our workers must give up these bad habits and customs. You are pointing the way for the masses to develop a new morality. These bad habits and customs are the mores of the capitalists. We are the revolutionary working class. How can we let ourselves be infected with these evils?"

Like Cu, Tu paid attention to straightening out our aberrations and passed on to us some very concrete struggle lessons. He told us of his experiences when mobilizing the masses and the workers in Bac-ninh, Ha-noi, Hai-phong, and other places. I felt those experiences were particularly helpful. Afterwards I also utilized Tu's experiences when mobilizing the workers at Phu-rieng to struggle with the enemy.

Brother Tu also pulled a few comrades out of Phu-rieng and other bases, trained them, then sent them to other plantations to mobilize the workers. His work kept him extremely busy. During the day he had his exhausting work as a coolie. At night, when he came home, he met members of the organization and cadres from various locations, to hear about the situation and to offer his opinions. Even so, he always had time to visit with people in the neighborhood and was highly esteemed by them. His mass stand was very good, and it was that fact that caused me to change many of my weak points and made me feel even greater affection for him.

Afterwards, when I was sent out to Con-son, I met Tu again. Being near him for so long I understood his spirit still better and had still greater faith in him and esteem for him. Then, a short time afterwards, he escaped from Con-son only to encounter a typhoon and be lost. I was depressed for months by the sorrow of losing Tu, my revolutionary mentor.[3]

Toward the end of 1929, Cu came to be suspected by the imperialists. The turncoat Duong Hac Dinh had fingered him, but because they did not have a shred of solid evidence, the imperialists could not imprison him. They deported him to the North.

The Phu-rieng branch gave me the responsibility of secretary. From then on I had to shoulder that heavy responsibility. It was a great honor, but I could not rid myself of the worry that, although I had been trained through years of struggle, I still did not have very much experience. All the same, I continued my activities with a firm spirit because of the uninterrupted liaison between me and brother Tu provided by the clever work of sister Ty, the worker with the big, round, deep black intelligent eyes who was so courageous.

THE HOUR BEFORE
THE STORM

From the time Vasser arrived, the capitalist owners softened their repressive policies. But it was only a matter of form rather than substance. They saw clearly that if they relied solely on beatings they could never force the workers to make great profits for them. Vasser now combined cruel beatings and pay docking with shrewd cajolery. He paid for costumes for the *cheo* group, for sports equipment, instruments, and drums. The party branch position was to take advantage of that opportunity to organize mutual aid associations, sports teams, and arts groups to bring the masses together and to win them over to us.

The workers formed three *cheo* groups in Villages 9, 3, and 2. As soon as they had a group set up, they would ask Vasser to allocate money to buy costumes and drums. The person in charge of all the *cheo* groups was comrade Quy, a member of the secret rubber workers union. Quy was active and very enthusiastic. He had a slight, slender build and an oval face, so that in the *cheo* plays he usually took female roles like Dieu Thuyen and Tay Thi.

Cheo plots were taken from ancient stories of *The Three Kingdoms* and *Heroic State of Eastern Chu*. At the time, each *cheo* group had as many as seven or eight plays. The most famous were *The Deception of Chou Yu, Pledge in the Peach Orchard, The Romance of La Bo and Dieu Thuyen,* and *Pham Lai and Tay Thi.*[1] In general the plays were self-written and self-produced, chosen with subjects emphasizing personal loyalty, filial piety, feminine virtue, and righteousness. We were not yet able to perform new plays with a revolutionary content, but those plays stimulated our patriotic spirit.

Every Saturday night, when the *cheo* drums sounded, the workers would come in great numbers from all the villages around. In the moments just before a *cheo* performance began, the executive committee of the labor union would skillfully guide the masses in new directions of struggle and explain the situation on the plantation.

In sports, we asked Vasser to let us start a soccer team. When evening came, the players took the ball out to the practice field. On Sunday they went out together to neighboring plantations for games. And there were many who went along to cheer them on. So while the players were contending on the field, the members of the labor union and members of the party branch were trying to make contact with the secret infrastructure from the other plantation to discuss the situation at the two places or to exchange experiences. And we took advantage of those times when team members went to Sai-gon for friendship matches to make contact with Ngo Gia Tu and to bring leaflets and secret newspapers back to the plantation.

We set up a dragon dance group, too. The group went around to all the villages on the plantation on festival days and at *Tet*. Members of the dragon dance group were all strong and healthy youth chosen from the Red Guards unit. They wrapped red scarves around their heads and wore red shirts. We were very fond of that color with its revolutionary significance. The dragon dance group practiced every evening. Taking advantage of that part of the dance where the dragon jousts with warriors wielding wooden weapons, the members of the group took wooden swords and staves and practiced the dance together. The truth was, we were practicing the martial arts all evening long. I was the "fighting master" who taught them to use the staves. Later, during the big struggles, the Red Guards were able to use sticks and poles well for this very reason.

We also organized mutual aid and assistance societies. When someone was sick, we would go to visit and take medicines. If anyone had the misfortune to die, we would take them out and bury them properly.

The non-Catholic workers had a Spring and Autumn society which, in keeping with the old customs, buried votive offerings to their ancestors or organized visits to shrines several times a year. Each time, they found a bit of wine and meat to set out for a pleasant meal together. The Catholics had a St. Joseph society. When someone died, the society would ask for a mass for them and pray for the soul of the unfortunate person. I was in charge of this society. Actually the religious activities of these two societies were very weak. They were simply legal mass organizations intended to bring together large numbers of people and to lead them to more advanced forms of struggle. We skillfully held on to the leadership positions of these public, legal organizations in order to smash Vasser's schemes of cajoling the masses and of trying to put them to sleep.

There were also the secret organizations, which included, besides the party branch which was the nerve center, a secret labor union and a unit of Red Guards. Comrade Hong, a party member, was secretary of the secret rubber workers union. Among the activists were Ta, Chuong from Ninh-binh, and Mo from Vinh-bao in Hai-duong Province. Chuong was later sent out to Con-son where he died of dysentery.

The executive committee of the labor union met once a month to assess the situation and to set out the general direction for the next month's struggles. The union published a monthly paper called *Giai thoat* [*Emancipation*]. There was no editorial board. Hong took direct charge of chasing down articles from members of the branch and from the union's executive committee. It was printed at night out in the forest by one of the workers. Although that newspaper was very rudimentary, duplicated by the gelatin block technique, it was quite practical and in close touch with the situation at Phu-rieng. Ngo Gia Tu himself praised the paper and liked reading it very much. The paper had columns on workers' daily activities and the union's operations. For international politics, it used excerpts from the Paris paper *Humanité*, and for news of struggles at home it carried selections from *Giai-phong* [*Liberation*], at that time the paper of the Indochinese Communist party.

When Tran Van Cung was arrested, the paper *Giai-thoat* carried an article in the name of the secret union demanding that the imperialists release him. Brother Cung was one of seven members of the Revolutionary Youth League who founded the first branch of the Indochinese Communist party.

Our union had a large membership. It could be said that an absolute majority of the workers belonged. It was indeed a broad-based mass, class organization of the party. The workers enthusiastically took part in its every activity. It was precisely because of this organization that the nerve center—the Phu-rieng party branch with less than a dozen members—was able to lead all the struggles there, from the smallest to the most massive.

The Red Guards were the party's armed organization. To be precise, the name of the group at the time was the Young Red Guards [*Thanh nien xich ve doi*]. I myself was the unit leader. In every village we organized a squad of about thirty people under the command of a squad leader. At the time the squad leader in Village 9 was comrade Nguyen Manh Hong, now [1971] deputy chief of the Forestry Service. Then, however, comrade Manh Hong was still quite young. From his short, plump, fair-skinned appearance, no one would have suspected that Manh Hong was an activist. And yet Hong worked irrepressibly for the party and his class, even though he had just turned sixteen. Hong and I were very well matched. Once I went to live for a month in Village 9 to talk with Manh Hong about our work. At night, like two brothers sharing the same bed, we fell asleep with our legs flopping one against the other.

The Young Red Guards had a very specific responsibility. They were the armed forces of the party branch and had the task of protecting the party and protecting the struggle. During strikes, the Red Guards always went along to guard the workers who were negotiating with the owners. In ordinary times, the Red Guards shielded the villages against the secret agents of the owners and the imperialists. These lackeys frequently hung around eavesdropping, spying on the workers to try to pick up news. Whenever the

Red Guards discovered one, they would beat him until he was barely able to crawl away, all the time shouting that he was a thief.

Discipline at that time was very strict. I devised rules for the members of the Red Guards unit to follow. Members had to pledge absolute loyalty to the party and the union and pledge to obey every order received. In dealing with secret agents, with foremen and with the owners, the Red Guards had to oppose them to the end in order to protect the workers' representatives, the members of the union executive committee, and the comrades of the party branch. All members had to give absolute obedience to their squad leaders and to the Red Guards commander. Besides that, the Red Guards were responsible for maintaining order on those nights when there were *cheo* performances and on days when there were soccer games.

All the Red Guards' activities were half public, half secret. As far as the owners were concerned, they were just workers like any others. From our side, however, the branch gave them every task which called for maintaining order and security, or for armed confrontation with the owners. I took advantage of the dragon dance group to teach them the martial arts. At the time, I did not even know the word "military," and had yet to give any thought to practice with guns, crawling and creeping as our soldiers do nowadays. The main thing we did was practice the dance with staves. I had always been quite good with staves, ever since the time I studied at the Hoang Nguyen seminary, so I now taught the others. Every festive day they took the dragon's head around to dance. They all appeared most imposing with red scarves wrapped around their heads, unbuttoned shirts tied at the waist with a sash, and staves in their hands.

The unit's weapons were still extremely rudimentary. We mainly used staves and hatchets. All these hatchets were simple tree-cutting tools, but they were forged of good steel. They were honed sharp and bright as a mirror, so it seemed that one light stroke would be enough to split an enemy's head right in two.

Since 1928, when Cu came to be with us, and especially since the founding of the Phu-rieng party branch, the workers' organization at Phu-rieng had grown tighter every day. Struggles were a lively mixture of legal and illegal forms. One of the first things we did was take a position of opposition to the docking of workers' pay and to corporal punishment. If someone was beaten, we took action immediately.

I still remember the incident when comrade Cao was hit on the head with a hoe by a French foreman because he had not finished clearing grass from an assigned plot of ground in time. All the workers laid down their tools. A hundred of us went to the manager's bungalow to present our case. The manager tried to pacify us. We did not listen, but continued our strike, demanding that the French foreman be expelled from the plantation and that the manager guarantee that workers would not be beaten any more. As for comrade Cao, we asked that he be given treatment until he recovered. While he was in the clinic and unable to return to work, the plantation was to continue to pay him. Our struggle was resolute. In the end the owners had to concede. We waited until they agreed to resolve the main problems before we returned to the work area.

Having won once, we pushed on to strike yet another blow. This time the union selected workers' representatives to go ask the manager to distribute good rice, meat that was not all gristle, and fish that was not rotten. The representatives argued that when workers ate such bad food, they became ill and could not go out to work. While the representatives were bargaining with the owners, workers who were sick with diarrhea, stomach ailments, or anyone of a hundred other diseases went to the nurse. It took about half an hour for each person, and since there was a total of at least one hundred people who came, the plantation lost scores of labor hours each day. The struggle thus had many facets, coordinated in tight synchronization. At first Vasser was unyielding, but after he had added it all up and seen that there was no way he could win, he resigned himself to resolving the problems we raised.

Gradually we pushed on to demand that women receive paid maternity leave and that rice be distributed to them while they were lying-in. Previously any woman who was giving birth and could not work was given no pay and no rice ration. Afterwards Vasser permitted them to receive two months' rice but still would not pay them, using the excuse that the contract did not provide for that. We did not yet press our demand for lying-in women to be paid. At that time there were struggles at many different levels. Sometimes only one group would strike, sometimes a team, and sometimes two or three villages stopped work at the same time. Vasser looked one way and then the other trying to find a way to deal with us. He made a show of going by the contract and sweetly proclaimed: "Whoever finishes early, come on back and rest, or play soccer and practice *cheo.*"

On the surface it sounded like a good deal, but in fact the terms of the contract he offered were quite harsh. The workers responded by doing their work in a plodding, evenly paced manner. If they were digging holes to plant trees, they would spread out in a long line across the work area, watching each other as they dug. Each person would wait until everyone else had finished digging a hole before going on to the next row. Thus the holes they dug wound up in straight lines with no one ahead and no one behind. The other tasks, such as planting saplings, clearing ground and hoeing, were done in the same way, with everyone keeping to the pace of the weakest member of the group. Not knowing what to do, Vasser was forced to reduce our quotas, and so we won. From that time on all completed their quota a half hour or an hour early, stopped work, and returned to take care of their private affairs. In short, we kept the pressure on Vasser so that he could not breathe easily. Every scheme, every artifice advanced by that renegade priest met with defeat.

One other thing needs to be said, though. In spite of our many victories, our daily life really did not improve a great deal. One detail will make that clear. Because of living conditions at Phurieng, all pregnancies resulted in stillbirths. Few women workers could carry their children even as long as the fourth month. That is sufficient to show what living conditions existed even then.

Gradually the rights we were able to demand increased. The daily regimen and the treatment at the clinic became less deplorable.

The owners had to buy more medicine and set up more beds. We struggled against the cruelest of the nurses until they were sent elsewhere. The workers who did the most strenuous work and grew ill were also allowed some injections of vitamins. And women workers could sometimes dare to come up to the clinic for examinations. The foremen did not beat us as much, and when they did, they dared not give such terrible beatings as they had in the past.

Then we advanced to the demand for hot water to drink while working. The clause concerning water was very important to us. At that time, when workers grew tired and thirsty, they would simply find a hole in the ground and drink the water standing there. In the bad climate, with so many malaria mosquitoes and a low level of sanitation, drinking standing water could be extremely dangerous. Malaria and dysentery were common at Phu-rieng.

We appointed a representative to demand that the owners assign one person in the morning and one in the evening to prepare hot water for the workers to drink in the work area. We had a very good rationale. With hot water to drink, the workers would not get sick; a full day's work would be profitable for the plantation; and the workers would benefit from improved health. Finally the owners had to go along. So every morning and every afternoon each work group chose one person to boil water for the group to drink. There was no shortage of firewood in the forest. And when someone was sick or feeling weak, they would be assigned to that job. In this way we were able to give an extra day's work to people who otherwise would have had to stay home from work without pay.

Vasser was on the one hand using blandishments and cajolery, and on the other hand making every effort to repress us severely. But he did not beat us in person the way Triai had. Vasser always used lackeys like the overseers Durandet and the LeBonne brothers. Durandet's beatings were no less severe than those of Monte. And he raped as much as Barre. Once he tried to make sister Nguyen Thi X from Thai-binh come to sleep with him. She refused. He laughed provocatively, then tied her to a stake and beat her on the buttocks. When he had finished beating her, he asked if she was ready to go with him yet, but she was still determined not to do what he said. He forced her down on the ground at once, then used a great bamboo cane to beat her dozens of times on the soles of her feet. When he got tired of beating her, he threw her back into the workers' village as one throws out an old torn rag. The flesh of her feet was shredded, and you could see the white bones in the mass of bloody, sticky flesh.

Durandet was in charge of Village 9, but he went out raping even in Villages 2, 4, and 6. To this day I still remember the stooped form of that deadly ape. In a fit of passion he would go through the rubber forest as the late afternoon sun's rays slanted down, searching for a mate, looking truly loathsome.

At that time the LeBonne brothers were still overseers for Village 9. The two were exactly alike in their faces and physical appearance and also in their temperament. The LeBonne brothers had heads fat and round as soccer balls, with red, squinting eyes and shiny, greasy skin. I do not know how long they had lived in Indochina, but they could sound off in Vietnamese like corn popping. They cursed and swore all the day long: "Mother fucker," "Father fucker"—the most despicable kind of profanity. As soon as the older brother finished beating in one location, the younger brother would come over with his cane on his shoulder. In the work area of the laborers from Village 9 you could always hear the sound of the LeBonne brothers quacking out their curses and the heartrending cries of those being caned.

While Durandet and the LeBonne brothers were beating the workers with such a vengeance, the manager Vasser shut his ears and pretended to know nothing. Whenever Vasser came out to the forest to watch the workers on the job, that crew just controlled themselves so that they seemed gentle as lambs. If they did get angry, they simply spoke testily. At such times, if a stranger were to come by, he would have thought that we could breathe easily at Phu-rieng; that laborers could work however they wanted; that the Vietnamese and French foremen did not beat or curse; and that the manager Vasser was as good as the earth, a carved silver crucifix with the figure of Jesus Christ nailed to the cross hanging around his neck. A stranger would have had the impression, too, that labor was carried out according to contract, that a worker could go back when he finished the work set out for him, that at night we could meet for *cheo* performances and other pastimes, and in the afternoon divide up for pleasant games of soccer. Phu-rieng was "heaven" indeed!

At the beginning of 1929, Michelin again changed the manager and some of the overseers. Vasser left and Soumagnac came. He was an air force captain, and even brought his French wife to Phu-rieng. Soumagnac was about thirty years old, a thoroughbred capitalist who owned many shares in Michelin. By this time the rubber forests at Phu-rieng had some trees which were almost three years old—nearly big enough for the first sap collection. The Michelin company felt they should select some trustworthy individuals with authority in the company to come oversee the work at Phu-rieng. Soumagnac met those criteria perfectly. He was a tall man and quite handsome. He always wore gold-rimmed glasses and spoke with a voice sweet as sugar.

In all of 1929 Soumagnac was only around Phu-rieng watching things about half the time. The other six months he took his wife off on pleasure trips to Da-lat, Sai-gon, Cap St. Jacques, and other places. Although he was seldom at Phu-rieng, we got a clear idea of what he was like. He was dissolute in some bestial fashion. He always had six or seven servants at his bungalow, as drivers, house servants, cooks, secretaries, and the like. Soumagnac selected each person with great care. They had to be handsome, strong, and young before he would take them. Any man who went to work in Soumagnac's bungalow had to spread his buttocks to satisfy the manager's carnal passions. Soumagnac kept this up until a person was haggard and pale, then turned him out and replaced him with someone else.

The wife took after her husband. Soumagnac's wife was only about twenty-one or twenty-two years old, devilishly beautiful and unbelievably passionate. She had a lover who was indeed a second

Paris. But besides her Paris, Soumagnac's wife made the servants and cooks come up to satisfy her, too. It could be said that as soon as the master belched, the mistress got hungry, and vice versa. After only two months workers who were called to serve in the bungalow were exhausted, their faces pale yellow, their bodies always warm and feverish, sweat drenching the backs of their shirts.

The assistant manager was this Paris who took care of the paperwork in the office, and who always clung to the skirts of Soumagnac's wife. Yet Soumagnac remained calm and let them be. The ethics, the morals of the colonialists were truly incredible!

The overseers under Soumagnac's authority still included Durandet from the old crew, and there was a man named Boudy who was in charge of Village 2. Boudy was famous for his cruel beatings. He would strike a blow which split the flesh of the person being beaten, bend down to examine the wound oozing blood, eyeing it like a craftsman inspecting his work, and then suddenly raise his hand and bring down another blow on top of the old wound, not a centimeter away, always keeping a perfectly straight face.

Under Soumagnac the method of setting quotas and the partially relaxed activities for workers continued as under the renegade priest Vasser. But by this time the policies of cajolery could no longer deceive us, no matter how treacherous they might be. Since 1929 Phu-rieng had had a Communist party branch. All the military executioners and renegade priests, all the policies of savage repression and two-faced cajolery mixed with torture, however cunning, had been unmasked.

We remembered when we had just arrived at Phu-rieng, the silence of the forests weighing so heavily on our hearts, making us homesick, causing us to long for our wives and children, stirring a hundred confused emotions. Everything was deserted, desolate, yet we had to live with this gang of beasts in human guise, who might beat us or bind us at any time. We had no way of knowing whether we would live or die.

But where there is repression there is struggle. The more savage the repression, the stronger the struggle. We rubber workers had resisted the capitalist masters right from the time we first left home. Were we to allow them to straddle our necks, tear out our livers and sip our blood?

In general, struggles such as those described above were aimed at demanding material benefits. They were primarily economic, but they also had clear political content. The workers of Phu-rieng had become a force, with tight organization, with leadership for struggle, with a head to direct it. It had all the characteristics of a self-conscious working class. This was clear evidence of the truth that a workers' struggle movement combined with Marxist-Leninist theory will give birth to a Communist party. After the founding of the party, the working class will advance from a "class of itself" to a "class for itself."

The Phu-rieng party branch had indeed guided the struggles from lower forms to higher forms. After the branch was formed, every struggle incorporated political slogans as well as economic ones. For instance, we demanded an end to the head tax, demanded release of political prisoners, and specifically demanded that Tran Van Cung be freed.

The more we struggled, the more we won. And the more we won, the more we struggled. The more we won, the more the masses believed in and gathered around the party branch. Gradually we learned to martial our forces, to protect ourselves when we were on the defensive, and to strike boldly when we were on the attack.

The movement had grown. By the end of 1929 it could be said that the party branch at Phu-rieng had the support of the majority of workers at the plantation. The others were also influenced by the branch through the broad membership of the union.

It was also at this same time that the whole movement of workers throughout the country was rising—weavers in Nam-dinh, cement workers in Hai-phong, workers in the Ben-thuy match factory, and others. The ferment was everywhere. The Phu-rieng party branch prepared for a new round of struggles to be waged on a greater scale as far as both ends and means were concerned.

It was right at this time that brother Cu was betrayed. The ruling clique deported him to the North. When Cu left, he turned over the task of secretary of the Phu-rieng branch to me. From that time I carried a heavy responsibility with virtually no theoretical understanding and with only a limited amount of experience.

THE 1930 STRUGGLE
OF THE PHU-RIENG
RUBBER WORKERS

Since before *Tet* in 1930 the Phu-rieng party branch had been making both material and spiritual preparations for the large-scale strike about to come.

From *Humanité* the branch learned that French workers making preparations for a strike paid great attention to the problem of food supplies. Studying that experience, the branch was careful to discuss and resolve the food problem before the strike broke out. To prepare for sufficient food supplies in case the strike should drag on for a long time, union members were instructed to set aside rice, salt, and dried fish. Each village selected a person to go into the forest, choose a well-hidden place, and make a shelter to hide the food. The cache had to be secure against rain and against plundering by rats or other vermin. In addition, it had to be safe from the eyes of the foremen and undercover lackeys of the plantation owners. The food stores were gradually built up over a period of months, a little bit each day. The branch also gave one unit of the Red Guards the task of finding some way to take over the plantation's rice stores when the strike broke out, then carrying the rice out to forest hiding places.

Hasty preparations were also made to secure weapons. Those in the blacksmith group at the garage machine shop used wrecked jeeps and automobiles to make a number of daggers and long knives for the workers. Whoever had a hatchet had to keep it sharply honed at all times. And each person had to make ready a sturdy pole and two torches.

The branch and the executive committee of the union also met many times to discuss the goals of the struggle. At the time, the workers at Phu-rieng had both common demands and particular demands for each village. For the workers of the plantation as a whole, the following rights were to be demanded:

- A prohibition on beatings.

- A prohibition on docking pay.

- Exemption from taxes.

- Maternity leave for women workers.

- An eight-hour work day, including the time spent going to the work area and returning to the barracks.

- Compensation for workers injured in accidents on the job.

In addition to these, there was one political slogan: Free Tran Van Cung.

There was another major point for the workers in Villages 2 and 3, those who had arrived in the same wave as I had. Those of us who had survived three years at Phu-rieng and were now about to complete our contracts demanded to be returned to our homes. The owners were to bear the cost of transportation and all other expenses. That was very reasonable and sensible.

At that time there were also a number of our compatriots from the mountain tribes who had been captured by the French and brought in to do forced labor. The French were absolutely merciless toward them. They were given only rice and dried fish and got no pay at all. We often had to help them treat intestinal worms and malaria, so the ties between us became quite close. Besides, I had already taken a vow with the oldest man in the village that we would regard each other as members of the same family. We definitely needed a positive response from them to our coming strike. We immediately talked to them about it.

They understood at once, and said, "Right. The big man makes us do forced labor for days, months, even years yet gives us no land to farm. And the big man gives us no money. The big man has taken all our land. Now we have to tell the big man not to capture us for forced labor any more. The big man must give us farmland so we can take care of our elders and children."

One person spoke to another. Finally they promised us that if the workers went on strike to demand that the big man give more money, they would also stay at home and not come to the plantation to work any more. And if the workers fled, they would show them the way through the forest. Taking advantage of the coming lunar New Year, they would quit work. They promised that if we kept them informed every day, then they would help us if anything happened.

We were quite moved by their sympathy for us. We warned them not to guide the French or join the French army. On the 27th day of the last lunar month we saw them off. They went straight back to their villages that night.

We were very happy with this response from the mountain people. Our struggle would not be isolated. When it became too fierce, we would have a place to take shelter. There were individuals among them who had been to lower Laos and even all the way to Thailand and knew the trails. If necessary, we could flee. In only one evening the hundreds of mountaineers brought in by the French for forced labor at Phu-rieng had returned home, every last one of them. That also meant that when our strike broke out, the plantation owners would not be able to find a single worker to replace us.

On the night of the 28th day of the last lunar month, the executive committee of the Phu-rieng rubber workers union implemented the party branch directive to call together in the forest a conference of representatives of the five workers' villages. A great many workers came to the conference. The meeting progressed in secret, but with great excitement and enthusiasm. A drizzle was falling, the night was black as ink, and the torches we lit were barely enough to illuminate and warm a small corner of the forest, far from the villages and barracks. The delegates sat around in clusters, shivering from the cold. Nevertheless, glancing around at their eyes and listening to their ebullient voices was enough to make one aware of the zeal of all of Phu-rieng. The major points proposed by the branch were all approved by the delegates. They accepted responsibility for returning to their villages and urgently completing tasks not yet finished.

The atmosphere in all the workers' villages at the time was very animated. Although the branch only intended to stage a strike, the workers prepared weapons as if they were getting ready for an uprising. There was a good side to that, but in another sense it was not correct, and one of our shortcomings was not to have resolved and calmed down that phenomenon in time. Indeed I must confess that in the bottom of our hearts we, too, were very moved by the tumultuous atmosphere. It was as if a tempest were about to break over the forests. Anyone who had witnessed how we workers were forced for all these years to grit our teeth, twist and turn, and endure the tyranny of the enemy would have found it hard to escape the kind of emotions I felt as I watched us now turn around and stand up.

The legal newspapers of the day reported that our strike began 3 February 1930, in other words the fifth day of the first month of the year Tan Mao [the Year of the Cat]. In fact our struggle began on the first day of the lunar New Year, in other words 30 January 1930. A few days before, the manager, Soumagnac, had gotten wind that something was about to happen. As we did not yet have much experience, our preparations were pretty much out in the open. Soumagnac had his lackeys pass the word to the workers to come up to welcome the New Year with him on the morning of the first day of *Tet*. Soumagnac said he would give everyone a bonus. He wanted to calm us down, to use the joyous atmosphere of *Tet* to buy us off. We used his lackeys to send word back to Soumagnac that on that first day we would indeed all come up to celebrate *Tet*.

And that's what happened. Beginning early in the morning, workers in all the villages formed up in ranks according to the directions of the Red Guards squad leaders and marched on Soumagnac's bungalow. They were boisterous but very well organized. There was no uproar, no jostling. Each person held a long staff ready in his hand.

In keeping with the customs at Phu-rieng during previous *Tet* celebrations, our dragon dance group led the way. The members of the dragon dance group were all fighters chosen from the Red Guards. Each had a red scarf wrapped around his head and red shirt and blue trousers belted at the waist by a sash. A group carrying clubs and hatchets went along on both sides to protect the dragon dance group. The farther we went, the longer the procession became. Each time we passed a village we gained several hundred more people. In the end, five thousand workers from all parts of the Phu-rieng plantation arrived in Soumagnac's front yard.

He knew something was happening, but he still made a show of bravery and came out to greet us from his veranda. His face still wore an arrogant expression and he puffed on a cigarette which dangled carelessly from his mouth. However, it was easy to tell from the way his green eyes darted about that his stomach was churning. There were so many of us, and the atmosphere was quite different from previous years.

Following our plan, the workers surrounded the yard and sat in perfect order to watch the dragon dance group. The group did all kinds of dances. The dragon's head, which we workers had made ourselves, was almost as big as a bed. Its tail was made of a number of widths of red cloth sewn together. It sprang around in the middle of the yard most energetically. The swordsmen and staff bearers made the dragon quake in fright. That day the swordsmen and staff bearers were able to do as they pleased, going up and down, back and forth freely. They displayed their fighting stances and their staves to their hearts' content. Every now and then a sword or staff came down, "whop," on the dragon's head, setting off a ripple of laughter in the crowd of spectators who encircled the scene so tightly. The beat of drums and the clash of cymbals went out to the rubber forest and echoed back again in unending waves.

When Soumagnac saw that we were doing nothing dangerous, he grew bolder and came a few steps down the veranda. He must just have finished drinking his fill of wine, because his eyes were as red as a fighting cock and he walked unsteadily, almost falling down. He spat out his cigarette, grinned broadly, and laughed along with the workers. We pretended not to notice him and concentrated on the dragon dance.

Soumagnac began in keeping with the custom of past years. He called his lackeys to bring in several money boxes and had them toss the coins out into the yard. He thought that the workers would scramble for the money as they always had in the past, presenting a spectacle for his enjoyment. But what happened this year angered and frightened him and made him lose face. One *hao*, two *hao*, five *xu*—they lay where they landed. Money rolled up to the workers' feet and lay glittering on the ground, yet no one made a move to pick it up.

The dragon dance team continued its dance, the dragon prancing around bravely and imposingly, quite different from the style of dancing in years past. It did not grovel on the ground, lick the earth, or bow and scrape in submission. On the contrary, like a courageous prince of the mountains and woods it jousted with the staff-wielding fighters. When it grew tired of jousting, the dragon turned to face the workers on every side and leapt into the air. We were so happy we shouted out praise to the dragon, then laughed and talked spiritedly.

Finally the dragon jumped across the yard, stamped on each *xu* and *hao* sparkling on the ground, then climbed up on the veranda of the bungalow. It flung out its white string beard, shook its head and wove back and forth majestically, as if issuing a challenge.

It was obvious from Soumagnac's face that he was enraged—something the workers found very satisfying. Soumagnac spread his arms and legs and signaled the dragon dance group to stop. He then used an interpreter to ask us, "Your master is good. Your master has given you a bonus. Why don't you take it?" The workers had already picked someone to stand up and answer, "It's *Tet* and we're just having a dragon dance for our own enjoyment. That's all." Soumagnac gave a flat little laugh, then offered us a *Tet* greeting, "In the New Year your master wishes you strength for your work, and your master will give you a raise!"

Then, according to the predetermined plan, comrade Hong, comrade Ta, and I gave Soumagnac a "*Tet* greeting" on behalf of the workers.

"Today, during the *Tet* celebrations, the master has wished us strength for our work. We thank him. For our own part we would like to offer the master our wish that this year may be even better for us. Let the master tell the foreman not to steal or dock our pay, not to beat us. When someone gives birth, may the master distribute rice to keep mother and child healthy. May the master not collect head taxes from us any more. For those who have already worked three years on the plantation and completed their contracts, may the master send them back to their fathers and mothers, their wives and children, their home villages. The master is good, so may the master ask the government to release Mr. Tran Van Cung because in the final analysis there is nothing for which Cung can be convicted. Now, in the spring, as one year ends and the *Tet* celebration heralds another year, we speak what we know, and we wish what we think. The master is good, so may the master do these things for us."

Thus, as if wrapping tough meat with some fat, we brought out our demands in the guise of a *Tet* greeting. Soumagnac was furious, but not in a position to do anything to us. He hemmed and hawed and promised he would consider the demands. After that, we started the thunder of the drums again, had another round of dragon dancing, then went noisily back to our quarters, leaving Soumagnac's yard glittering with coins. The manager was very frightened and humiliated! Never before had he seen such "*Tet* greetings." Our show of strength triumphed, especially on the spiritual level. We all returned laughing and talking noisily, some people mimicking Soumagnac's long-faced, dumbfounded expression when he saw that not one of us was going to scramble after the money he had thrown out. The workers also recalled the demands we had made in the guise of a bittersweet "*Tet* greeting," then fell to discussing them heatedly.

During the three *Tet* holidays, as intended by the party branch, the union stepped up its efforts to weld the workers more firmly together. During the day, groups of workers went around visiting each other; at noon and in the evening they cooked and ate together. At night, when the drums of the *cheo* group or those of the dragon dance group sounded, workers came together to watch in great numbers. Taking advantage of the time before the curtain opened, representatives of the union got up to speak to the workers. The gist of their speech was: "Why is our life so harsh? We must join our hearts, unite our strength so that we can demand the right to life." Thousands of workers as one gave their enthusiastic support. We unfurled the hammer and sickle flag. This was the first time the flag had made a public appearance before large numbers of plantation workers. The workers gazed at the flag in admiration. The color of the flag was bright red, like the hot blood coursing through the workers' veins at that very moment. The hammer and sickle emblazoned in gold on the flag were the very tools they used every day. It was indeed the proletarian banner.

That speech, as well as other activities of the party branch and the union, had considerable impact on the workers' spirit of struggle. Their sense of unity grew, and they realized that if they united closely they would become a great force.

The owners did not fail to notice this. They sent their lackeys out to stick close to us and gather information. But these secret agents were grabbed by the Red Guards and beaten half to death. The Red Guards accused them of thievery, seducing the girls, fomenting trouble, and all manner of crimes as excuses to give them a suitable thrashing.

At that time there was one union member in Village 2 who fell sick and died. We organized a very large funeral for the unfortunate man. Taking advantage of the large assembly, the union also selected a person to say some parting words for the deceased, and to raise the question: "Why did he fall sick and die?" The French, sensing the danger, intended to block the proceedings and disperse the crowd. But we would not agree, and in the end they had to allow us to continue our activities.

Over the three days of *Tet*, the union disseminated the strike order to the workers. The union advised: Stay where you are; whenever the owners agree to deal with our demands, the union executive committee will announce it and you should then return to work. Everyone agreed enthusiastically.

On the morning of the third day of the New Year, the French blew their whistles until their mouths were tired, but except for a few scattered lackeys, the workers did not turn out for roll call. The French foremen decided to prod the workers into going to work. Wherever they went, though, they encountered blazing, determined eyes. The foremen were so frightened that they all withdrew to the manager's house and turned their lackeys loose to spy around.

One of the secret agents at the time was a man from Bac-ninh who was working as a nurse in Village 2. He was hanging around eavesdropping when brother Lu caught him. Comrade Lu was a foreman, but he stood on the workers' side. He was big, with a fiery disposition and real enthusiasm for the struggle. When Lu caught this secret agent eavesdropping, he beat him up on the spot. And when the agent escaped and ran, Lu chased him all the way to the manager's house. When the French foremen saw all the commotion they poured out of the house. They caught Lu, accused him of thievery, and imprisoned him.

When we got the news, we passed it to all the other villages. At once a wave of tumultuous indignation spread through the plantation. Thousands of workers stormed toward the office. They shouted for Lu to be released at once. The demands which had been put forth on the first day of *Tet*, which the manager half-heartedly promised to consider, were presented again forcefully and urgently.

Soumagnac closed his door and did not dare come out. The workers encircled the place and shouted until the heavens shook. Throughout that afternoon and night, and even into the next morning (the fourth day of the New Year), they still did not loosen their ranks. The Red Guards assigned people to stand watch, and the rest all lay down right on the grounds of the manager's house to sleep and thus preserve their strength. Villages 9 and 10 were so far away that it was eight the next morning before they arrived. With these added forces, the struggle spirit of the workers grew. Thinking the struggle had spread, the wood-gathering and land-clearing groups even farther away abandoned work and came in. The signal drums sounded, passing the message from one village to the next, calling anyone who had been left behind to come to the manager's office.

The tempest had risen at Phu-rieng! Five thousand long-suffering workers had arisen. They had completely surrounded the manager's compound, and at intervals they would call out for satisfaction of the demands which had been put forward. The turbulent struggle atmosphere frightened Soumagnac. He blanched, bolted all the doors carefully, and secretly telephoned the military outpost at Phu-rieng to bring in soldiers and free him from the encirclement.

When the colonial government received the news from Soumagnac, they were no less panicked. The commander of the outpost tried to find some way of overpowering the workers quickly. At ten in the morning a French soldier led twenty-five red sash troops into the plantation. They first encountered a group of workers who had just finished work and were coming to the manager's office to join the struggle. The soldiers decided to block this demonstration and disperse it before moving to repress the workers surrounding Soumagnac. The French soldier raised his gun and threatened them: "Halt right there! Making trouble, are you?" A group of women at the head of the demonstration continued their advance. The Frenchmen shouted, "Disperse at once! If you don't, the master will fire! You must listen to the master!"

But no one paid the slightest heed to his threats. They kept moving straight ahead, noisily, with an extraordinarily strong spirit. The Frenchman ordered his soldiers to fire into the air to threaten them. At the sound of the guns the workers, including many Red

Guards members, excitedly pounced on them. Some flung sand into the eyes of the soldiers so they could not see. Others used staves to fight them. One particularly determined woman put both arms around one of the soldiers, wrestled him to the ground, and took his gun. The Frenchman raised his gun and aimed it straight at the crowd to fire, but one Red Guards member sprang toward him, struck him a blow with his staff and broke the man's hand. The Frenchman cried out, "Stop, stop, don't strike the master! The master will not shoot any more!"

The remaining soldiers fled as fast as they could. Their uniforms in tatters, they ran like ducks to their trucks and sped straight to Sai-gon. Our workers captured seven assault rifles and took five prisoners of war. They then freed the captured soldiers, but shouldered the guns to take them to the office.

The news that the soldiers from the outpost had been defeated was transmitted at once. The workers sent up a joyous shout. Growing excited, many people rushed straight to the house where the manager and foremen were hiding and pounded noisily on the door. Soumagnac was so frightened that he had to open the door and negotiate. We selected Hong and Tu as representatives. I was also in the delegation, but the workers asked me to keep my role secret. Comrades Hong and Tu raised the demands previously decided on. No sooner had they stated a point than Soumagnac accepted it, not daring to hesitate in the least. The declaration was signed at once, with the workers' representatives on one side and Soumagnac on the other, representing the owners. The delegates held the declaration high in the air and announced to all the workers that the negotiations had brought victorious results. Cheers echoed in all directions, and many people jumped to their feet shouting. In the face of that scene, the manager and foremen pulled their heads back into the house and did not dare utter a single word.

The first step of the struggle was victorious. The owners had been forced to accept all the workers' demands. Our experience in struggle at that time was only sufficient to help us operate at that level. The union gave the order for the workers to disperse. The excited workers spilled across the roads and returned noisily to their villages.

We organized a demonstration which marched from the manager's house through the plantation. The party members and union executive members went at the head of the procession. Next came the women workers' group with three hundred sisters, followed by other workers from all ten villages. The Red Guards, shouldering the seven rifles they had seized from the soldiers and another dozen or so bird guns they had confiscated at the office, marched on both sides to protect the demonstrators. From time to time they sent a shot booming into the air.

The demonstration continued. We raised the hammer and sickle at the head of the column, and the strains of the "International" resounded from our ranks:

"Arise, ye prisoners of starvation,
Arise, ye wretched of the earth . . ."

People impoverished and enslaved had indeed arisen. Some of the foremen who had signed on half-heartedly in the past came out to join us, too. When we had finished the "International," we sang another revolutionary song to the old tune "*Hanh van*":

"Our suffering is too great, my worker friends!
To live we must take our turn,
Clear out this path of chains,
Make it resound with our labor.
Too long have we borne this life of grief and tragedy,
We shall not endure such tyranny forever.
The party is our teacher, the farmer is our friend,
Join strength, unite hearts,
On this field we shall topple
Even the French authorities and Southern Court.
With all our might we shall fulfill
Our destiny as workers.

We shall topple tyranny
Throughout the five continents.
This life must quickly be smashed
And socialism founded,
So we may hope for equality and freedom."

The owners of the little variety stores, who were related in a roundabout way to the wives of the Frenchmen, were so frightened that they hung up strings of firecrackers in festive fashion and lit them to placate us. But the demonstrators paid no attention and continued to wind their way from one village to the next. Whenever the demonstrators reached a broad clearing, they stopped. A comrade from the party branch or a comrade from the union executive committee would locate a mound of earth to stand on and make a speech. We still had no theoretical understanding. Whatever one person said in one place, someone else would repeat a little later. And yet the audience would be entranced, not the least bit bored, and the speaker would raise his voice until he was hoarse.

After that, we went back to Village 3, where the owners had set up a rather large sawmill. There was a strong fence around the mill. The French overseers hoped that if they took refuge inside, they would be able to escape the storm that had beaten so fiercely about them these several days. The Vietnamese overseers tagged along to hide there, too.

But they did not realize how strong the workers' movement at the mill was. The leader in Village 3 was comrade Doanh. A number of workers had been planted inside the sawmill in advance, to act as a fifth column. When the demonstration approached, the French overseers were very frightened. They had guns, but did not dare fire them for fear they would meet death at the hands of the masses. They ran back and forth in the millhouse, grumbling and fussing at one another.

The people who rushed in most enthusiastically were the Red Guards, including members of comrade Manh Hong's unit. The gate to the mill was locked tight. They grabbed the gate and rattled it, causing a great commotion. Several boosted each other up to scale the fence. But right at that moment the undercover comrades inside the sawmill picked up boards to use as weapons and gave the French overseers such a beating that they were dazed and tattered. One of the overseers had his arm crippled and later had to go to the hospital in Sai-gon. Then one of the workers inside unlocked the gate. As the gate opened, a mass of people cascaded into the mill. The French were so terrified they raised their hands in surrender. We captured more than a dozen guns, both field rifles and hunting guns, then returned in orderly fashion to Village 2. The auto garage was there along with the generating station and the water plant. The water plant was quite large, with a very tall concrete water tower. We rushed in and seized it, too. Actually, there were no Frenchmen guarding these places.

We then split up into several wings. One wing went to take over the tree nursery. At the nursery there was a storehouse for tools, including a large number of hatchets and tapping knives which could be used as weapons. Another wing went to capture the rice storehouse. Once we captured the rice stores we considered our victory complete. As they marched, the workers carried the hammer and sickle flag, raised their guns and hatchets in the air and shouted slogans. Now and then they sang a song and fired several shots in the air as a show of force. As the rays of the late afternoon sun slanted down, we went back to the plantation office. With spirits riding high, the workers rushed into the office and captured it as well.

Now the whole of the Phu-rieng plantation belonged to us. The manager, the assistant manager, the chief foreman, and his subordinates had all been defeated at the time we dispersed, then went back to organize the demonstration through the plantation. Every last one of them slipped away. Their houses and offices were completely deserted. We broke into the office desks and flung all the contracts out in the yard, where we made a bonfire of them. We threw out all the work records and burned them, too. Watching the flames leap high into the air, we thought that this would erase every trace of our slavery, and that from then on we would be free!

Those were unforgettable moments. I was elated. In my life of revolutionary activity there were three periods which were most exciting to me: the day of struggle when we seized power at Phu-rieng; the days of the August 1945 Revolution; and the days when the Resistance triumphed in 1954.

That day in Phu-rieng I remembered Marx's teaching: "When the proletarians struggle, they have the whole world to win. They have nothing to lose but their chains." Indeed the vast Phu-rieng area was completely in our hands. That so intoxicated us that we did not yet take the measure of every dimension, we did not yet look beyond the plantation to the state of the revolution in the country as a whole. I must confess that our level of awareness at Phu-rieng at the time was such that we could not possibly see that aspect clearly.

Intoxicated! It was pitch-dark before everyone remembered that no one had put so much—as a grain of rice in his stomach all day long. So, with torches ablaze, the masses of people followed the leading comrades and the demonstration made its way back to the food stores. As we went, we sang and shouted slogans which penetrated deep into the forests.

When we arrived at the storehouse, we opened it and took out the rice and dried fish. We slaughtered several of the plantation's cattle at one time. The cooking units set about their work. The *cheo* group prepared a presentation. When the food was done, it was brought out on trays, and we began a truly bountiful banquet to celebrate our victorious *Tet*. When the banquet was done, we went to see the *cheo* performance. That night the group presented a story very appropriate to the spirit of unity among the thousands of workers at Phu-rieng. That was the tale *Pledge in the Peach Orchard,* which tells of the life-and-death spirit of brotherhood of three men, Liu Pei, Kwau Yu and Chang Fei, at the time of the Three Kingdoms.[1] The performance drew enthusiastic applause.

Actually, I only heard about the performance later, because while the workers were so intoxicated with joy, the party branch was holding a special meeting in a small shelter behind Village 3. Only there, far from the seething atmosphere in the middle of the plantation, far from the voices shouting slogans, the guns firing into the air, the revolutionary slogans, did those of us in the branch finally calm down and assess the situation in a more clear-sighted way.

The meeting was very tense and continued throughout the night and into the morning. There were two lines put forward, diametrically opposed to each other.

One was to fight back if the enemy brought troops in to terrorize us. We would fell trees to block all the roads leading into the plantation. Red Guards with their captured guns would be stationed at the most critical points. The rest would be assigned to patrol duty, to guard the food stores, and to guard the generator and the water plant. This line corresponded to the psychological inclination of the majority of the workers at the time. That very night, after they returned from watching the *cheo* performance, the workers divided up on their own initiative to prepare weapons. Some gathered up sacks of kitchen ashes to fling in the faces of the soldiers, others refitted their hatchet heads more firmly in place. The Red Guards members taught each other to fire the guns, because the fact was that the majority of them knew nothing about how to shoot. They thought very simply and very heroically: "What difference does it make if we live or die! If they come tomorrow, we will fight. If we fight, we will fight to the end." We could well be proud of that aggressive spirit.

The second line was advanced by a minority that included me. I said, "The party has not yet directed us to seize power. If we seize power, we must do it at the same time throughout the whole country. That way enemy units will not be able to rescue each other. If Phu-rieng rises up now, all by itself, the enemy will bring in troops to terrorize and repress us. We must change the direction of our struggle to avoid defeat."

When this line was first advanced, it drew vehement protests. Those who agreed with me made every effort to convince the others. We emphasized the need to preserve our forces and to preserve the lives of the five thousand workers at Phu-rieng. "The imperialists are savage," I said. "Once they have marshaled their forces, they will not hesitate to wipe out all five thousand of the virtually unarmed people here." We also recalled the bitter defeat following the violent killing of Monte the year before.

We had to contend with the opinion that such a course of action was cowardly and demonstrated base fear of the enemy. To counter the arguments of those who were ready to risk their lives in a round with the enemy to prove their honor and heroism, we had to use the [Chinese] classics to explain: "Know thyself, know thine opponent, and a hundred battles will produce a hundred victories," and, "The hero must know when to advance and when to withdraw: to advance when he can fight effectively, to withdraw to preserve himself...."[2]

After an internal struggle which lasted most of the night, the branch finally agreed on a course of action. The comrades divided up to go to all the villages to explain the new line. It took another round of fierce convincing before things were settled.

Implementing the branch's directives, the Red Guards took all the captured guns and lined them up beside the manager's office. As we had previously decided, the union carried a quantity of rice, fish, and salt to hidden storage sites in the forest. This would guard against the enemy's cutting off our rations. The workers dispersed and went back to their own villages. The struggle continued, but we were simply on strike.

So that the new line would be implemented well, we worked hard to explain, to convince, and to train the workers in methods of struggle which would be legal to the imperialists. Gradually the workers understood, but because we had exposed ourselves so much, the lackeys infiltrated among the workers' ranks by the imperialists had a clear understanding of the activities of the comrades in our party branch and labor union. Because of that negligence—a product of our lack of experience—the enemy dealt us a number of defeats.

The enemy began to mobilize their forces to deal with us on the morning of the fifth day of the New Year. That afternoon, two buzzing "old widow" airplanes hovered for hours in the air over Phu-rieng, both to study the situation and to assert their authority over us. The next day the *Résident* of Bien-hoa, Marty; his assistant, Vilmont; the Governor of Cochinchina, Krauheimer; and the head of the Indochina *Sûreté*, Arnoux, came up to Phu-rieng along with twenty trucks carrying three hundred legionnaires and five hundred red sash troops.

A few kilometers from the plantation they got out of their trucks, organized the troops and, guns at the ready, rushed into the plantation along several different paths. The imperialists were clearly determined to wipe out all of us the moment we tried any adventuristic resistance. But they "missed the boat." Wherever they went, they saw nothing but workers going about their lives as usual. Workers also lined up and sat in orderly fashion listening to our representatives debate with the imperialists.

The Governor, Krauheimer, bellowed a question at us: "Do you know why it is that the masters have had to bring troops and guns up here?"

Comrade Hong, who was our public representative at the time, stepped forward and replied, "We have no idea!"

"We have had to bring the soldiers in because you were rioting!"

"Not true! When were we rioting?"

"The manager said you beat him, beat his soldiers, and stole their guns!"

"The manager is not telling the truth! He himself has had people beat us to death many times. We have called on the government to investigate and to tell the manager not to beat us or dock our pay, because otherwise we suffer a great deal."

"Call on us if you wish, but how dare you stay at home instead of working?"

"We've been appealing forever, but the manager has not listened; we're so hungry and tired we can't go out to the work area!"

"You're lying!" the *Sûreté* chief, Arnoux, said threateningly. "How was it you stole your masters' guns?"

"That's not true! We don't know what it was the soldiers were afraid of, but they abandoned their guns and fled. The guns are still here!"

We pointed to the guns lined up against the wall. The colonialists were at a loss what to do. Their intention was to bring big, brave, strong soldiers up to Phu-rieng, thinking it would be like using sharp steel to fight a snake. They did not expect to encounter a jester. With no excuse to slaughter us, they withdrew and busily consulted with each other for a long time. In the end the imperialists had to tell their interpreter to tell us, "The master instructs you to return to your villages. Early tomorrow, if you go to work without any trouble, the owners will treat you well."

The workers dispersed in good order. However, taking advantage of the moment, the lackeys the enemy had earlier infiltrated among the workers fingered a number of individuals to Arnoux so he could arrest them. The enemy took them to the trucks, intending to leave. At once five thousand workers turned around and clung to the sides of the trucks, struggling with the legionnaires to hold onto their fellow workers. They said, "The masters just said they were good and that we should return to our places, but now the masters are arresting our men. If you want to arrest someone, arrest all the thousands of us. We will all go to prison!"

The workers struggled quietly but very firmly, and in the end the French were forced to free the arrested men.

The legionnaires and red sash troops had to withdraw from the plantation shortly after that because we had secretly removed the impeller from the water pump. Without drinking water for so many troops in the middle of the forest, they had to pull back to Bien-hoa. In the end, the troops went all the way back to Saigon. The troops at the Phu-rieng outpost were given a platoon of reinforcements. The French withdrew their troops, but they left behind a great many secret agents.

The owners of the plantation subsequently used the pretext that there was very little rice in the storehouse and distributed it only to those who went to work. The goal of this action was to use the discipline of hunger to break the strike. Thanks to the rice previously taken out to the forest, however, the workers remained in their village as before, and the strike continued.

But immediately afterward, because of our inexperience in secret activities, and because of our intoxication the day the struggle burst out, the majority of comrades in the party branch and the executive committee of the labor union were betrayed. Because the masses had not yet been trained carefully in clandestine activities, secret agents were able to uncover clues about us. The owners knew that if they wanted to break the strike, they would have to aim their blows at the strike's nerve center. So they used one excuse after another to arrest our comrades. One by one, in various circumstances, comrades Ta, Hong, Hoa, and the others fell into the hands of the enemy. Eventually my turn came, and I was discovered while propagandizing some mountain tribe soldiers on the Phu-rieng plantation. In my pocket at the time was a leaflet with the hammer and sickle flag printed on it. Using every trick they knew, the enemy also uncovered the printing service out in the forest, complete with paper and ink and the ditto gelatin. As they continued their arrests, they rounded up hundreds of others.

Parallel with this flood of arrests of cadres and active members of the movement, the owners also had to concede a number of the demands they had signed. They distributed good rice, they improved some of the conditions of treatment at the clinic, and they promised that they would allow those who had fulfilled their contracts to return to their home villages.

Thus a number of our demands were implemented. At that point the struggle ended for the time being. The struggle had tightened the ranks of the workers at the Phu-rieng plantation, and had given the people who remained additional training in legal and semilegal struggle, as well as secret operations. That tradition of struggle would continue to develop at Phu-rieng. The victorious struggle had given the brothers and sisters increased confidence. The workers at Phu-rieng elected a new leadership committee to replace the responsible comrades who had been arrested by the enemy. By May of that year—in other words only three months later—another struggle burst over Phu-rieng on a scale no less large and determined than the first one in February.

THE RED SEEDS
OF PHU-RIENG

The struggle at Phu-rieng broke out when the guns of the Yen-bai
uprising had just fallen silent, and it broke out during the period
when our [Communist] party was being founded. This fact is evidence that our party had a strong tradition of struggle, for when it
was just being formed it was able to lead such imposing struggles.[1]
It also shows that from 1930 on the leading role in the Indochinese
Revolution in general and the Vietnamese Revolution in particular
was exclusively in the hands of the proletarian class and their party.
Indeed, tumultuous workers' and peasants' struggles had broken
out in Ha-noi, Hai-phong, Nam-dinh, Vinh, Bien-hoa, Sai-gon,
and other places at almost the same time as ours at Phu-rieng.

The struggle at Phu-rieng had widespread repercussions. At
the time, however, each stratum, each class evaluated it differently.
While we were imprisoned, the wrapping papers on some of the
presents sent to us by friends and relatives included some daily
newspapers. Thanks to that fact we were able to learn of the reac-
tion to our struggle. *Than Chung* [*Common Spirit*], a progressive
paper of the day, discussed the Phu-rieng strike in its issue of 10
February 1930, under the headline, "The Rebellion at Phu-rieng."
The article said:

> Was it because of Communist influence?
> Eight hundred coolies fled into the jungle, a hundred
> ringleaders were arrested, and the rest will be sent back to their
> home villages.

Who says it was easy to quell! The bloodshed and smoke have been halted, but the waves of suffering continue. The furious workers have rebelled, and yet, in the words of the office manager at Phu-rieng, and in the words of the French technical journals, it was because of Communist influence. And so, after the coolie band had beaten up two policemen and wounded them seriously, it immediately sent spokesmen to talk with the office manager to request:

- An eight hour work day.
- The expulsion of two French foremen.
- The release of a foreman who had been arrested.

This foreman, named Luu,[2] was arrested for theft, as we said before. The manager said he had no authority to release him, so the workers would not work and all returned to their Village 9, where they raised two red flags over the camp.

Red flags! Such a suspicious sign! So the French went out to inspect. They arrested a hundred people who they thought were at the head and trucked them back to Bien-hoa. And 800 coolies in Village 9 fled into the jungle. They fled from the French and went to meet the savages, heedless of hunger and thirst and wild beasts. They say that hunger had driven even the wolves from that jungle. Can this be so? And then the people from Village 3, with only three months left on their contracts, came to ask to return to their home villages.

Among the suspects arrested at the plantation was a medical orderly of very gentle mien,[3] and yet the *Sûreté* found in his pocket several tiny pieces of paper with a crossed hammer and sickle at the top. As the arrested people stated, these propaganda leaflets were scattered by some strangers who came up to Phu-rieng by car from somewhere or other. They were carefully printed, and in the dialect of the North. That is the reason the authorities said they were certain the communists had their finger in the affair. It could not possibly be a wild goose chase. Indeed?

Over a hundred police and ten French gendarmes, plus the *Sûreté* agents from Thu-tich and Thu-dau-mot, were enough to preserve order and security at the office and to present a show of force to frighten the workers.

The fuse on the gunpowder which exploded these past few days was not spun out of thin air. The manager said he had noticed that for about the last month the workers were doing a better job than before. However kind he might have wanted to be, he could not escape it. The capitalists and the workers were on a collision course.

Things are quiet now at Phu-rieng.

That is the complete text of the article. Although quite a number of points are incorrect, it is still possible to see from the article that:

- Because the repression and exploitation were too great, Phu-rieng had to struggle.

- Although the imperialists arrested hundreds of people, they still had to satisfy a number of the demands of the workers, including their aspiration to return to their home villages. Thus our struggle had been victorious.

- The party had skillfully changed the course of the struggle so that the scheme of using the discipline of hunger to force the workers to return to work did not succeed.

This was the opinion of a number of progressively inclined petty bourgeois intellectuals who wrote for the paper *Than Chung*. As for the imperialists, naturally they tried to distort the incident and slander us in every possible way, labeling us thieves, rioters, troublemakers, and such. The fact was that in their first collision with an extremely flexible kind of struggle, the imperialists were disorganized and responded very passively. They arrested hundreds of people and imprisoned them at Bien-hoa, and because of that the echoes from Phu-rieng reached even farther.

In the past, the prison at Bien-hoa had held only common criminals. The prison guards beat these prisoners savagely. They had no sleeping mats and their rice, mixed with lime, which had a strong odor and gluey texture, was eaten with squid. Now they locked up the hundred-plus brothers who had been arrested at Phu-rieng and treated them in the same way. The head of the prison guards was a tall, gaunt man with a long, dark face. He was very cruel and talked in the most vulgar way. We called him the "horse's mouth." Accustomed to the old ways, the horse's mouth went on with his games of cursing and beating us. Imagine his surprise when a hundred people protested. We went on a hunger strike and used the old tactic of shouting and raising a ruckus. Some people started clanging pots, pans, and butter tins together. The racket could be heard as far away as Bien-hoa town and disturbed the population so much that they came out to see what was happening. Finally the prison director had to come to us and negotiate. We argued with him and demanded sleeping mats, hot rice, and hot water. We demanded to be treated as political prisoners. The director was surprised to see how serious and courageous we were, quite different from the sort of prisoners he normally dealt with. He admired us. In the end he had to forbid the horse's mouth to wander into the political prisoners' cell block.

The common criminals also admired us greatly. They whispered to each other, "What these secret society men say is really right, really admirable." After that, whatever we did, they also did.

The Phu-rieng trial was a large one, in which hundreds of people were sentenced. It was also one of the first trials of Communists. In the past those who were tried for their political activities were village scholars, mandarin idealists, and intellectuals. This was the first time "coolies" had formed a secret society. For that reason the Phu-rieng trial attracted considerable attention. Knowing this would be the case, the rulers plotted to shame us. According to their law, before a person is convicted he has the right to wear his own clothes and does not have to wear the numbered prison uniforms. But we workers had no clothes. Each of us had only a pair of shorts and a tattered scrap of shirt. In the struggle with the soldiers when we were arrested, the shirts were shredded even more. We entered prison half-naked.

As the day of the trial approached, the French flung in to us a bundle of tattered clothing. They thought that if we went to court with such a shabby outward appearance, we would have no status at all. We could guess the rulers' plans. We told each other, "There are bound to be many people coming out to watch when we go to court. We must do something to make them admire us." We thought that if we had really neat clothes, we would wear them. If not, we would wear whatever we had. The most important thing was to remind each other to maintain a serious, stalwart demeanor.

On the day of the trial more than a hundred of us formed up in ranks of four to go from the prison to the court. There were soldiers leading the way, soldiers bringing up the rear, soldiers escorting us on both sides, but we prisoners walked firmly, each person wearing nothing but a pair of shorts. As we marched, we sang songs we had learned while we were at Phu-rieng. The songs resounded through the streets. People standing to watch from both sides of the street cried. I still remember one very old woman standing on one side of the street who brought her hands together in a gesture of greeting, her face screwed up in an expression of anguish, who said, "Good heavens! You gentlemen who work for the country must suffer so much!" Seeing such an old woman express her sympathy stirred us deeply. If the masses respected us and felt such affection for us, we must behave in such a way that they would not be disappointed. As this thought sank in, our enthusiasm rose.

When we reached the court I argued on our behalf. The chief magistrate said, "You have violated your contracts by refusing to work. That is disturbing the peace."

"We have acted quite correctly," I replied. "It is the company which is in the wrong. They have beaten people and given them too little to eat. They have killed innocent people without cause. It is they who have violated the law."

The court whispered, and people in the gallery said to each other, "Look at these workers arguing so forcefully." Finally the judges handed out sentences indiscriminately, five years in prison to some, three years to others. We protested noisily.

On the road from the court back to the prison we again formed up in ranks of four, as if for a demonstration. Some sang, some shouted slogans. The atmosphere was very enthusiastic, and no one showed the least anxiety about their prison sentences. So we gained the affection of the people of Bien-hoa. In admiration they lined both sides of the street waiting for us to march past on our way back to the Bien-hoa prison. This parade of the Phu-rieng workers singing songs and shouting slogans had great influence.

The workers at the Bien-hoa sawmill were preparing to strike at that time. Our trial encouraged them to step up their struggle. The leader at the Bien-hoa sawmill at the time was brother Lien, who later met me on Con-son and said, "Because of your inspiration, we were all the more enthusiastic about our strike." (When the August 1945 Revolution triumphed, Lien became chairman in Hue and later gave his life during the resistance.) The comrades in Bien-hoa distributed leaflets in their factories protesting the unjust sentences given to the Phu-rieng workers.

Our trial was later taken to the appeals court in Sai-gon. On the last day of the trial, large numbers of people came out to watch. When they saw us singing and shouting so strongly as we walked, they were quite surprised. They praised us, saying, "Wearing sarongs like that, they can engage in politics?"

When it came time for arguments before the court, we represented ourselves. The chief magistrate was from Pondichéry, a French colony in India. "You are guilty of disturbing the peace," he said. "Do you understand your crime?"

"How can I be guilty?" I remonstrated. "Look at me in my rags and tatters and half-starved! The Michelin company has not lived up to their contract. They have shortchanged us on our pay. They have beaten us. It is they who are guilty, not we."

"All right, all right, Michelin is going to take care of the pay and the beatings," the chief magistrate said, then questioned us threateningly, "but who put you up to this rioting at Phu-rieng?"

"Who put us up to this? It was the French government that put us up to it! It was Joan of Arc who put us up to it! I ask you, since you are an Indian, do you want India to be independent?" I answered straight into the chief magistrate's face, so that he was stung and his face turned purple. The spectators were silent. Taken aback, the chief magistrate took out his handkerchief to mop the sweat from his face, but did not say a word. After that the judges withdrew to their private chambers. When they returned to give their verdict, the chief magistrate avoided looking at us.

At this time they passed sentence on dozens of us. Another comrade and I were to be sent to Con-son for five years. Three people were sentenced to two years in prison. Among them was comrade Manh Hong. At the time, Manh Hong was not on the union executive committee, nor had he yet been inducted into the party branch. All the same, the imperialists had a deep grudge against him because they knew that Manh Hong was famous in the struggle and that he himself had commanded a number of Red Guards youth in the attack with staves which had left their soldiers in such a shambles. There were also more than a dozen others sentenced to six months or a year in prison.

The trial inflamed public opinion at the time. The imperialists called it the rebellion of the plantation coolies. Their pen-wielding servants followed this lead. They published the results of the trial under headlines intended to discredit us. One said, "Phu-rieng Plantation Workers Riot." Another said, "The Disturbance at Phu-rieng." But they could not blindfold public opinion. Large numbers of Saigonese had gone to the trial. They were very surprised when they saw us going back proudly to prison after the sentencing. As we went, we sang the song, "Our suffering is too great, my working friends," and when we finished singing, we shouted slogans. Our whole bare-chested, sarong-clad brigade marched solemnly through the streets of Sai-gon, our heads held high, unafraid, unintimidated.

Although the imperialists wanted to picture us as rioters, our attitude and our actions showed clearly that we were political activists. Afterward *Than Chung* carried a report on the trial. The article concluded with the sentence, "And now the time has come when the poor are engaging in politics."

After that I was shipped to Con-son Island. This was the first of the many imprisonments in my life as a revolutionary activist. It was my first semester in the "University of the Revolution." At Con-son I lived with Tong Van Tran and Ngo Gia Tu, my two revolutionary mentors. I also met Ton Duc Thang, a mature Communist, a sailor who had been in the impressive struggle on the Black Sea.[4] By this time Uncle Ton was already getting on in years. He regarded younger prisoners like me as younger brothers. He felt very sorry for us and shouldered all the heavy, difficult work. I also met my other comrades and close friends in struggle.

The others sentenced at the same time I was were exiled to Ha-tien. The imperialists forced them to do hard labor and gave them only the sparest of rations. The workers could not stand it and struggled spiritedly. The imperialists had to move them to another location. That year comrade Manh Hong was only seventeen years old. The imperialists sent him to Ong Yem, a camp reserved for juveniles, which was like the French reformatory for juveniles in the North in the past. At Ong Yem the imperialists were also clearing forests to plant rubber trees. They even exploited the labor power of the detainees at the Ong Yem camp. Manh Hong was already experienced in struggle, and he still held fast to the hot-blooded struggle temperament he had shown at Phu-rieng. So Manh Hong became the leader of the struggle at Ong Yem. The imperialists had to segregate him and exile him to Con-son.

I still remember the day in 1932 when Manh Hong and I met again on Con-son. We were so happy we could not stop talking. We lay down side by side and recalled our experiences in the struggle at Phu-rieng. We grew even closer together than we had been before.

All our comrades on Con-son were very interested in the struggle at Phu-rieng. I still remember how Uncle Ton, Le Van Luong,[5] and a number of other comrades criticized us for knowing how to advance and how to withdraw, but not knowing how to defend. This lesson was most appropriate for the workers at Phu-rieng.

We knew how to attack, and we knew how to pull back at the right time, but we did not yet know how to organize to preserve our forces. The more I reflected on it, the more I saw how right they were.

For my own part, I was still anxious to know what the results of our struggle had been. I often asked myself about that. But events answered this question for me. At the end of 1930 the news reached Con-son that the northern workers who had come to Phu-rieng at the same time I did had been allowed to return to their home villages as promised in the contract. At the same time, the rubber workers at neighboring Dau-tieng plantation were mounting a large strike.

Uncle Ton called me over and said, "See, these are the results of what you youngsters did at Phu-rieng." These two bits of unexpected good news made Manh Hong and me very happy. We embraced each other for joy.

And it was true that, although a number of party members and union cadres had been arrested, the Phu-rieng struggle was not in vain. The imperialists were forced to concede many of our demands. Developing that tradition, and learning from the experiences of that struggle in early 1930, the struggle movement at Phu-rieng from then on was very good. Workers from Phu-rieng, nurtured in the furnaces of that struggle, became resolute cadres and party members after they fanned out to other places around the country. The red seeds of Phu-rieng were indeed excellent seeds.

I think back on the time when I left the Hoang Nguyen seminary, when I was but a patriotic farm boy. I was troubled and ashamed at the loss of my country, but at an impasse, unable to find the course to take. It was precisely at that time that the party sought me out and helped me to see clearly what course I should follow. The party directed me to proletarianize myself. The party taught me to integrate myself into the working masses. And so I had gone to Phu-rieng. Under the imperialists, Phu-rieng was indeed a hell on earth. Yet where there is repression, there is struggle, and the harsher the repression, the stronger the struggle. The suffering workers of Phu-rieng had thrown off the yoke of oppression and stood up. From the first scattered, spontaneous struggles they moved into a new period, under the leadership of the party. Those struggles were a powerful awakening, and they achieved some initial victories.

I was challenged and forged in those struggles. From being so immature and inexperienced, thanks to the party's training in struggle I matured, along with the rubber forests of Phu-rieng. After Phu-rieng, the party trained me on Con-son to become a person who was useful to his class and to his people.

Afterwards the course of my struggles led me to Ha-nam, Ninh-binh, Ha-dong, and Viet-bac, then to the prisons of Nam-dinh, Ha-noi, and more. However many places I went, I still remembered Phu-rieng, that corner of the rubber forests which turned into a red zone at the time of my training in struggle, the training which forged me as a member of the Communist party.

November 1964

Notes

INTRODUCTION

1. Pierre Brocheux, "Le Prolétariat des plantations d'hévéas au Vietnam méridional: Aspects sociaux et politiques (1927–1937)," *Le Mouvement Social* (Paris), no. 90 (January–March 1975): 63. The Great Depression reduced the number of contract laborers to 10,800 in 1933, but five years later the figure had risen to 17,022.
2. Ibid., pp. 71, 80.
3. *Nhan Dan* (Hanoi), 12 February 1967.

A FORK IN THE ROAD

1. At that time the main progressive writings were by Liang Ch'i Ch'ao (China), Phan Boi Chau, Phan Chu Trinh, and the Dong Kinh Nghia Thuc group. Their work was generally known as modern literature. (Footnote by Ha An, from the original text.)
2. Westerners referred to Vietnamese as "Annamese" until at least 1945. The term "Annam" was also used in a narrower sense to distinguish central Viet Nam from the north ("Tonkin") and the south ("Cochinchina"). Partly because the term meant "Pacified South" as coined originally by the Chinese, partly because of derogatory colonial remarks such as recalled here by Tran Tu Binh, most patriotic Vietnamese avoided using "Annam" or "Annamese" after about 1930.
3. Actually, the height of the movement was in late 1925.
4. The new governor general of Indochina, Alexandre Varenne, arrived in the middle of this campaign, which also included cables from Vietnamese and French groups in Paris.
5. Phan Dinh Phung led resistance to the French in central Viet Nam for a decade in the late nineteenth century. De Tham opposed the French off and on for nearly thirty years by various means in the mountains of northern Viet Nam until his violent death in 1913.
6. Phan Chu Trin died of tuberculosis in Saigon 24 March 1926.

7. King Khai Dinh attended the Marseilles Exposition of 1922.

8. The author refers here to the Vietnamese Marxist assessment that Phan Chu Trinh was too reformist, too nonviolent in approach compared to Phan Boi Chau.

9. The common English translation is "Thou shalt not bear false witness."

10. The Vietnamese *sao* is about 360 square meters, so the plots described were less than one-tenth of one hectare.

11. *Nom* was a complicated form of character writing, adapted from Chinese characters, developed by the Vietnamese many centuries earlier to represent their own phonetics and syntax.

12. Later, however, the author notes that he also could read some Latin and speak some French, which placed him ahead of at least 95 percent of the population and was of no little significance when dealing with the colonial enemy.

13. Tong Van Tran subsequently led the first successful escape from Con-son Island, in 1934. However, he was recaptured a year later and apparently died under torture soon thereafter. See: Thep Moi, "Tong Van Tran," in *Guong Chien Dau cua Nhung Nguoi Cong San*, Hanoi, 3d ed., 1965, pp. 53–73. Also in *Nhan Dan* 1037–1039 (6–8 January 1957).

14. The French-owned Bata corporation produced several types of simple molded rubber shoes and sandals in Indochina.

15. Established by Ho Chi Minh in 1925 as predecessor to a full-fledged Communist party.

THE ROAD INTO HELL

1. The retail price of rice in 1927 was about 8 *xu* per kilogram. A laboring adult would need at least a half kilogram of rice per day, plus vegetables and a bit of fish sauce.

2. Equivalent to graduating from primary school.

HELL ON EARTH

1. Or 0.40 *dong*.

2. The green sash around the waist identified district or provincial militia units, whereas the red sash was for regular troops who could be moved anywhere in the colony or around the world.

3. Presumably the author is referring here to the Protracted Resistance of 1945–1954.

4. The Viet ethnic majority.

5. He is now deputy chief of the Forestry Directorate—Author's note.

The First Battles (1927–1928)

1. Tran Tu Binh's details on maltreatment of Vietnamese rubber workers and the retaliatory killing of Monte are remarkably similar to information contained in three letters sent to the Viet Nam Independence Party (*Viet Nam Doc Lap Dang*) headquarters in Paris in 1928 and publicized in a subsequent handwritten pamphlet. A copy of the undated pamphlet is in the Archives Nationales de France, Section Outre-Mer (Paris), NF 645.

2. The *cheo* is a centuries-old dramatic singing medium popular in North and North-Central Vietnam. While the stylistic rules of *cheo* poetry are complex and firm, the subject matter is open and the mode of presentation spontaneous. Generally, both tragedy and ribald humor are projected in each play.

3. *Than Chung* was a daily newspaper published by Diep Van Ky and edited by Nguyen Van Ba. It was started 7 January 1929 and closed by government order 22 March 1930.

4. Actually, Khai Dinh had died in 1925. The French brought his son, Bao Dai, back from the metropole (France) briefly for crowning in 1926, then sent him off again until 1932.

5. There is some question about Bui Bang Doan's exact status. Telegraph cables from the French governor general to Paris in 1930 cite mortality figures gathered by a "controller of hand laborers" named Bui Dong Doan, almost surely the same man. See Pierre Brocheux, "Le prolétariat des plantations d'hévéas au Vietnam méridional: Aspects sociaux et politiques (1927–1937)," *Le Mouvement Social* (Paris), no. 90 (January–March 1975): 71.

The Party Comes to Phu-rieng

1. Ngo Gia Tu was born of a peasant family in 1909 in Bac-ninh Province in northern Viet Nam. He was an energetic trade union organizer for Ho Chi Minh's Revolutionary Youth League in the late 1920s. At a May 1929 meeting in Hong Kong, however, he split with the leadership over the question of when to establish a full-fledged Communist party. Returning to Viet Nam, Ngo Gia Tu moved with others to form a party. This position was vindicated by the majority of league members, including Ho Chi Minh, at the Hong Kong unification meeting of February 1930.

2. The Buoi school took its name from the Ha-noi suburb in which it was located. The French called it Protectorate College. After the August 1945 Revolution the school was renamed for Chu Van An, a

prominent Confucian literatus and private schoolmaster of the Tran dynasty (1225–1400).

3. Further information on Ngo Gia Tu is available in *Vietnam Courier,* April 1975, pp. 21–25.

THE HOUR BEFORE THE STORM

1. All the presentations recalled here by the author are on historical themes, an endless source of inspiration for the *cheo. The Deception of Chou Yu* and *Pledge in the Peach Orchard* are taken from particular episodes about military heroes in *The Three Kingdoms,* a popular Chinese novel about events of the third century A.D. *La Bo and Dieu Thuyen* is a love story involving a general and the heroine of the novel. *The Heroic State of Eastern Chu* is another Chinese novel which, like *The Three Kingdoms,* was translated into *quoc-ngu* (romanized Vietnamese) in the early twentieth century. Pham Lai and Tay Thi are the two principal characters in a third novel.

THE 1930 STRUGGLE OF THE PHU-RIENG RUBBER WORKERS

1. See note 1 in previous chapter.

2. These strategic concepts date back to the writings of Hsün-tzu (third century B.C.) and Ssu-ma Ch'ien (first century B.C.) in China.

THE RED SEEDS OF PHU-RIENG

1. Presumably, the author does not refer here to the abortive Yen-bai uprising (9–10 February 1930), which was led by the Viet Nam Nationalist Party (Viet Nam Quoc Dan Dang).

2. This Luu was really comrade Lu—Author's note.

3. This medical orderly was Tran Tu Binh himself—Note by Ha An.

4. This refers to the protest which took place in 1919 among sailors aboard French warships sent to help crush the Bolshevik Revolution. Back in Viet Nam in the 1920s Ton Duc Thang was one of the labor union organizers, particularly at the French arsenal in Sai-gon. He is now president of the Socialist Republic of Viet Nam.

5. Le Van Luong was later to be prominent in the land reform campaigns of the 1950s and to take some responsibility for party errors. He is now a member of the Political Bureau of the Central Committee.

CPSIA information can be obtained
at www.ICGtesting.com
Printed in the USA
LVHW100756220723
752714LV00001B/1

9 780896 801196